D0897995

KEATS

From the Life-mask in the National Portrait Gallery.

KEATS

A STUDY IN DEVELOPMENT

BY

HUGH I'ANSON FAUSSET

ARCHON BOOKS
1966

To

PERCY WITHERS

FIRST PUBLISHED 1922

REPRINTED 1966 IN AN UNALTERED AND
UNABRIDGED EDITION BY PERMISSION OF
MARTIN SECKER & WARBURG, LTD.

LIBRARY OF CONGRESS CATALOG CARD NUMBER: 66-13341
PRINTED IN THE UNITED STATES OF AMERICA

FOREWORD

THIS short study of Keats, developed from a review
contributed by me to the *Times Literary Supplement*
at the time of the Keats' Centenary, is an attempt to
trace the steps by which the poet defined and
purified his perception both of life and of art.

A close examination of Keats's poetry in the order
of its composition, and of his letters in relation to
his poetry, revealed to me a very logical and significant development from sensationalism to vision,
from idealisation to idealism.

This gradual definition of his genius, once grasped,
should give new point to all he wrote. It makes us
more completely one with the intimate dilemmas,
the vast potentialities of his abundant nature. His
personality, viewed in its struggles for light and for
more absolute expression, symbolises too the everlasting duty of art, and his poetry in all its changing
detail ceases to be fortuitous, and reveals an organic
unity, to which each particular poem contributes a
part, representing a step or a stage in the direction
of that absolute goal for which we discover Keats to
have been aiming.

Continual ascent towards an ultimate harmony, an
impassioned creative truth, is the desire of all poets
most worthy of the name. But the processes of that
ascent, except in the work of Shakespeare, have

rarely been traced. Most men are content to accept in a poet's work, without enquiry, what immediately appeals to them, and reject the rest without questioning its significance either in itself or as an expression of a stage in the poet's experience. Few read great poetry as the testament of a vivid personality, as a life document, the stirring history of an arduous search for higher truth and purer beauty, as the relative evidence of an absolute revelation. This has been my aim in this short chronological treatment of Keats's poetry. His was such a rich, human, and universal personality as repays so close a scrutiny. And the details of his spiritual development drawn here from a study of his poetry may be doubly reinforced by any reader intimate with his incisive Letters, those passionate confessions of a natural, self-examining genius, quick to detect the cant of sentiment either in himself or others.

In one such genius as Keats, the whole problem of art and life is concentrated; in tracing the growth of his mind we follow intensively the course of civilisation, the development of men's conception of beauty, the gradual enlargement of their spiritual consciousness. So intimate a study has not to my knowledge been attempted before, and to many who read poetry indiscriminately, for the immediate unconsidered returns of pleasure, it may seem at first sight gratuitous. They see no need to follow a poet step by step, living anew his experience. Keats's rich sensationalism and luxurious artistry is enough;

the human problem, the unresting pursuit revealed in his poetry of ever purer beauty and more absolute truth, seems to them a metaphysical foible, abstract and beyond the concern of art.

Yet it was upon this problem that all Keats's rich energy was more and more consciously concentrated; a philosophy of life, as distinct from a mathematical system of thought, the work of the metaphysician, is the whole concern of a great poet. Without such a central principle, implicit in all his feeling, a poet can only weave pretty patterns, versify moral sentiments, or twitter like a bird. And without our recognition in him of such an aim, slowly defining itself through experience, both his poetry and his life lack unity and complete significance.

This latent principle inherent in all Keats wrote, and at last concisely expressed in the recast of Hyperion, I have attempted here to trace. It is the story of a soul discovering itself through the senses, of a mind adjusting its powers to balance the energy and greed of the appetites. In that balance Keats realised the central truth of life. He put himself into harmony with the creative mind of the universe, he entered the kingdom of Heaven; his human soul in its passionate love rose above the elements of force and the frailty of the flesh.

In such a balance lies the only hope of the world.

NEWTOWN,   H. I'A. F.
    NEWBURY.

> " The awful thing is that beauty is mysterious. God and the Devil are fighting there, and the battlefield is the heart of man."
>
> DOSTOEVSKY : *The Brothers Karamazov.*

THE appreciation of Keats has had a curious history. Initial disregard was followed by an over-emphasis of one quality inherent in his genius, and even dominating it for a large part of his brief life, a quality which was for all that only conditional, attributable to his youth more than to his determination, and receding, or rather transforming itself, as his powers developed.

This quality was his sensuousness, and an incomplete understanding both of Keats's own character and of true aesthetic values led the enthusiastic to admire and exalt above all else those of his poems which Keats himself discredited even to the point of unfairness, while it enabled the puritanical to condemn or criticise his nature on false premises. It was in this way that the Pre-Raphaelites indulged their own romanticism by sentimentalising a delicate fragment, *The Eve of St. Mark,* and disregarding a gigantic torso, *The Fall of Hyperion,* while censorious critics, specialising on Keats's love of claret and the mythical peppering of his tongue, on " O for a life of sensation rather than thought," and on the letters to Fanny Brawne, emphasised their own exquisite refinement by depicting Keats as

9

something of a languid aesthete, with the passions of a Cockney, the mind of an apothecary, and the vulgarity of the lower classes in the conduct of a love affair. We have possibly exaggerated both the snobbery and the condemnation, but even Arnold, while he drew particular attention to other strains in Keats's temperament, wrote of the love letters: "We have the tone, or rather the entire want of tone, the abandonment of all reticence and all dignity, of the merely sensuous man, of the man who is 'passion's slave.' Nay, we have them in such wise that one is tempted to speak even as Blackwood or the "Quarterly" were in the old days wont to speak; one is tempted to say that Keats's love-letter is the love-letter of a surgeon's apprentice. It has in its relaxed self-abandonment something under-bred and ignoble, as of a youth ill brought up, without the training which teaches us that we must put some constraint upon our feelings and upon the expression of them. It is the sort of love-letter of a surgeon's apprentice which one might hear read out in a breach of promise case, or in the Divorce Court. The sensuous man speaks in it, and the sensuous man of a badly bred and badly trained sort."

The pedagogue in Arnold, as we see for all his protestation, could not resist the temptation of a homily. And it is not with the abstract sense of this that we disagree, so much as with its tone and with the application of a particular principle of conduct to an individual in peculiar circumstances, and that individual a poet. The Victorian age did not understand passion. Its own art production is proof enough of that. It worshipped sentiment, however vague or conventional, but the manifestation of a primitive force of desire was a spectacle which it was too cultivated, too removed from either crude or inspired reality, to comprehend or condone. It desired its artists to sacrifice truth (if a sacrifice had to be made, though it would not for itself recognise the necessity), to the manners of a Victorian gentleman. To mistake the voluptuous for the beautiful is doubtless an error, but an error, in a poet of Keats's stature, to be attributed by preference to the immaturity of genius rather than to social inferiority or a neglected upbringing. For a true genius belongs to no class.

The Romantic Movement symbolised in the early years of the century a great liberation of sense even more than of mind. And in England at least after the first four great protagonists of this emancipation had passed, the elemental passion of the impulse failed. It degenerated into sentiment, that is into a condition when both mind and sense functioned on a lower, less primitive and less active level, on a level in which the values recognised were not those of a life of ultimate and universal perfection, but those of a social creed and a social conscience. We see this element of falsity or arbitrary limitation of the truth increasing as the century

advances, we see it inciting men of bolder genius to
resist it and exaggerate their own sincerity in a protest against complacence, such men as Swinburne,
and Meredith, and for a later example, John David-
son, and we see the original idea which moved so
potently and insatiably in its first brief lease of un-
restricted life, sinking through the sententious, the
elegant and the fanciful into the sickly or arrogant
condition of self-absorption, which marks the last
decade of the century, when poetry pretended with
the desperation of old age to a passion which it had
not the emotional or mental strength to support.

Keats belonged to the early period of ample exult-
ant passion.   He was sensuous, philosophic and
acutely intellectual, and all with a keenness which
sprang from an eager appetitie for life, an appetite
undulled by academic learning, a curiosity un-
fettered by the artificial restraints and attitudes of
what Arnold calls " good-breeding."   He was in
short a genius, young in a young age, a time

> " In which the meagre, stale, forbidding ways
> Of custom, law and statute took at once
> The attraction of a country in romance "

and his genius in its creative activity was of necessity, to begin with, undifferentiated: he sought
beauty with all the ardour of instinct, snatching at
light in the darkness, responding everywhere with
almost too rich a sensibility to the pure sensation of
life.   His thought, in Wordsworth's words, was

steeped in feeling, but both the thought and feeling were coincident only with the bounds of life itself. Self-criticism came, as the developing mind took more and more part in the creative process, and as Keats in uncreative moments submitted the impulses and experiences of his instinct to progressive analysis, translating his sensations into thoughts, and after deepening and amplifying the thoughts, reinterpreted them in the language of sensation.

We purpose here to trace through Keats's poetry, chronologically considered, the stages by which he purified his imaginative insight, by which in fact he advanced from sensationalism to idealism. It is not necessary in our time to refute that earlier tradition which sacrificed the strength of Keats's character, and the acuteness of his intellect, to an elegant dis-- taste for his sensuousness and his passion. Sir Sidney Colvin, truly " a jealous honourer," who combines the accuracy and liberal learning of the scholar with the sympathy of a magnanimous human being, has made all of us so familiar with Keats's person and circumstances, that we and our posterity could never fall again into such an error of prejudiced misunderstanding. We have only to scan his picture to know Keats the man, as he was in all his inspiration and distractedness, to know the character, aims, and passions, in short the pure natural being, of one in whom we feel great spirits to be sojourning. Yet neither Sir Sidney Colvin's admirable " Life," nor Professor de Sélincourt's agreeable erudition avail to bring us into absolute contact with that secret soul struggling after ideal expression, which we can only discover for ourselves after long intercourse with the poetry itself. They can disentangle the material forest of conditioning circumstances and show us the main paths, but every poet can be viewed as a personality reacting to circumstances and as a soul striving for truth: as a fact limited by fact, and as a fact striving to be an idea. It is true that Keats was by nature so devoted to life that his human concerns bear a close relationship to his poetry. But in the latter aspect the poetry, uncomplicated by notes or circumstantial exegesis, remains as the only ultimate evidence, the nearest, if the most difficult, bridge between us and another soul, as it was the last barrier between the poet and the silence which expresses all, the glass ever varying in colour and substance, through which the white light of eternity strove to shine.

ii

Again, a summary of Keats's attitude towards either life or his art at any given point is likely to be more misleading than enlightening. That Keats attained to perfection of its kind in the *Eve of St. Agnes*, for example, is not of so much import to us, as that he tasted the bitterness of frustration in *Hyperion*. For Beauty no less than thought has its mounting scale of values, its degrees of reality,

14

and to accept perfection on one level as undistinguishable from perfection on another is to betray the reason.

> " That low man seeks a little thing to do,
> Sees it and does it :
> This high man, with a great thing to pursue,
> Dies ere he knows it."

We must pass through all the stages by which Keats struggled towards the ideal, honouring his excellence or admitting his failure in each, before we can claim to know him, or dare to offer him the tribute of our appreciation.

For the value to us of a great poet, no less than of the whole history of man and the arts, lies in his continual advance, in his struggle to refine upon his vision and embody it anew, or to widen his horizons. The ascertainable facts of Keats's life are now widely known, but the philosophic understanding of his poetry, the metaphysical problem, if we may dare the invidious phrase, has tended towards neglect in an unqualified acceptance of the plastic beauty of his art.

His creative life was tragically brief, but it was concentrated and intense, and his imaginative development was correspondingly rapid. His very virtue, that which held out such high and ultimate promise, only for death grievously to disappoint, that too which offended the nice taste of our grandfathers, was the fact that his being was steeped with life. He, endowed with the potentialities of heaven, was so gloriously of earth, so richly embedded in it. There was no danger that his idealism, vital as it was, should end in the smoke of metaphysics, the fog of moralising, or the elemental mist that drifted in such immaterial beauty about the peaks and caves of Shelley's world. The Beauty which Keats adored, the perfection for which he came more and more to hunger, the misery which he realised, were drawn out from the life of nature and of man by one who was intimate, as no other poet perhaps save Shakespeare has so completely been, with the desires, the impulses, the needs, the potent limitations of both. He was drenched in naturalism and in that sense of kinship with common humanity by which we cry " Abba Father." This naturalism, uncriticised except by the unconscious taste native to his young personality, is the foundation of all that followed; it is to be accepted as the original clay from which each later vessel is modelled and re-modelled; it survives, though with how great a difference, in the last line of the second version of *Hyperion* as in the first of *I Stood Tiptoe upon a Little Hill.* Yet naturalism contains within itself the germs of all philosophy; beneath the predominating instinct, the apparently spontaneous impulse towards attractive sensations, the mind is functioning all unknown. Thus all the characteristics of a genius are generally to be found lurking in his earliest utterance; they exist there undefined, and still to be estimated at their true worth. But a poet in his

development does not adopt from outside new
qualities : he only revises the value of those qualities which he possesses, and adjusts their relationship to serve the purest imaginative purpose. Thus
instinct, reinforced and enlarged by mind, becomes
intuition, and mere sense-perception becomes
spiritual vision; so that acute physical sensibility is
the necessary prelude to the subsequent intellectual
understanding, which images its ideas through
passion. In Keats's first poem we find both his
surrender to and close observance of nature, his
mystical sense of something higher than nature, and
his human sympathy, the three forces with which
his mind and instinct were to struggle to the end.
But they exist there only in luxurious confusion.
The first impression therefore is of a wide and eager
sensibility, nurtured too on the second-hand experience of literature more than on a direct intimacy
with nature; and exercising itself in luxurious arti-
fices, interspersed with moments of true sincerity.
But even in this period when fancy is extemporising
on fancy, the dominant quality is an appetite for
pleasure, an unappeasable sensuousness, and this
passive joy of sense is the same force, expressing
itself in grosser values, as the joy of spirit out of
which pure beauty springs. That Keats's sensibility
had responded at first by choice to luxurious and
fanciful art is significant of his temperament, which
was passively receptive to an unusual degree. We
can trace this tendency to langour and sloth through

most of his poetry; it is evident, as a recent writer
has noticed, in his love of stillness, and even more
apparent in the worst vices of his style, in his lapses
into sickly voluptuousness and sugared vulgarity,
and in his false attitude to women. But it was only
a virtue uncontrolled, the feminine quality of recep-
tivity for a time more powerfully resident in him
than that male quality of assertion, which inevitably
increased with the growth of his mind. The com-
pany of Leigh Hunt, and his particular study of
Spenser, Fletcher and Chatterton exaggerated the
disproportion, which is the clearest sign of his immaturity in the Poems of 1817. Certainly his first
creative effort was not so much that of active desire
as of surfeited sense, compelled in its own interest
to rid itself of absorbed and crowded impressions.

> " I was light-hearted
> And many pleasures to my vision started,
> So I straightway began to pluck a posey
> Of luxuries bright, milky, soft and rosy."

His garden was indeed too full, the soil was too
fertile, and he plucked that there might be space for
other flowers to grow and other sweets to be tasted.
This is a general definition of his genius at that time;
the particular instance, notably the Chapman sonnet, might seem to contradict it. But nothing is
more typical of a young natural genius than its
capacity for attaining the heights of imagination
coincidently with the most abysmal depths of vulgar

sensationalism.   The whole Elizabethan age is an example of it.

The true appreciation of Keats's original genius and its first development is to be drawn from studying together *I stood Tiptoe upon a Little Hill* and *Sleep and Poetry*.   In the one

> " he seemed
> To common lookers-on like one who dream'd
> Of idleness in groves Elysian."

In the other his languid satisfaction with the physical universe, with the rich limitations of sense, not successfully disguised by mere indulgent lip-service to spiritual conceptions, is at least partially disturbed by active recognitions of an infinite region, where great forces move, and by the self-imposed task of realising their truth and of bringing their truth and so their comfort home to humanity.   *I stood Tiptoe upon a Little Hill* is as remarkable for its moments of unconscious inspiration as for those of unconscious flaccidity.   We have the two in direct contrast in the following:

> " And when again your dewiness he kisses,
> Tell him, I have you in my world of blisses :
> So haply when I rove in some far vale,
> His mighty voice may come upon the gale."

But such weaknesses and such powers are only significant in so far as they reveal instinct in its moments of assertion and acquiescence, as passively

limited by space and so reflecting nature's vulgarity
in human terms, or as in the full tide of organic life
and so echoing the language of the torrent or the
storm. Keats's attitude to nature is the important
thing to note. He watches intently Nature's "gentle
doings," and like Pope, he records the external
spectacle of life with a perfect exactness, whether

" Where swarms of minnows show their little heads,
Staying their wavy bodies 'gainst the stream "

or

" the soft rustle of a maiden's gown
Fanning away the dandelion's down " ;

or of the moon

" lifting her silver rim
Above a cloud, and with a gradual swim
Coming into the blue with all her light."

The argument of the poem is that Nature is the true
inspiration of poetry, and Keats instances the
natural allegory of the Greek myths, of which he
holds the tale of Endymion to be " the sweetest of
all songs." But this reaction from the artificialities
of the previous age, more definitely asserted, as we
shall see, in *Sleep and Poetry*, is in itself still an
artifice, and an attitude. Keats does not understand
Nature, he merely takes languid pleasure in her,
observing her with the eye of the connoisseur, and
feeding on her with the refinement possibly of an
epicure, but too often with the appetite of a gourmet.

KEATS

" For what has made the sage or poet write
But the fair Paradise of Nature's light ? "

is a happy cliché; it has all the half-truth of an
epigram.

" In the calm grandeur of a sober line
We see the waving of the mountain pine "

is a moment of enlarged sense, when perception has
seized on an analogy and expressed it finely. But

" And when a tale is beautifully staid,
We feel the safety of a hawthorn glade;
When it is moving on luxurious wings,
The soul is lost in pleasant smotherings "

is a combination of mental conceits and indolent
sensuous vagueness. It is this ignorance of reality,
this idle pasturing on the vegetation of life, that
enables him to describe a natural phenomenon, " a
lovely sighing of the wind, Along the reedy bank,"
with rich and exquisite appropriateness, but also
leads him in his innocent inadequacy of mind and
experience to describe things of infinite potency,
whether of physical anguish or of spiritual ecstasy
in " words of honey," to write of " sweet desola-
tion," or " balmy pain," or of those supernatural
beings

" Shapes from the invisible world, unearthly singing
From out the middle air, from flowery nests,
And from the pillowy silkiness that rests
Full in the speculation of the stars."

If his spirit wandered at times, it did not soar; for the most part it lay enfolded in his avid senses, which absorbed life greedily, or still oppressed by his mind, which in its moments of activity gave precise definition to the matter seized upon by the senses, or interposed with its own clever conceits. Nature, humanity and a supernatural region are each recorded here, but objectively or superficially. He never identifies himself truly with any of them, and the moon which was to be a symbol to him almost as potent as it was to Shelley, appears as a decorative illustration. We find in the poem a degree of cunning, a luxuriance often profligate and uncontrolled, and little truth or sincerity.

A great advance in effort and understanding is registered in *Sleep and Poetry*. Keats had already escaped the limitations of Leigh Hunt. He had turned not only to Shakespeare and Wordsworth in literature, but in critical sincerity to Nature herself. There is evident both a profounder if inconsistent consciousness of human values, and a corresponding improvement in the power and purity of his expression. He had quickly ceased in fact to see life as an exotic spectacle, women as nymphs in tapestry, and virtue as the mock chivalry of a Calidore. He had realised that poetry implied not pleasurable indulgence but a passionate struggle for truth, as it imaged itself in beauty. His realisation was still far beyond his conscious capacity, and his lapses into sensationalism were still frequent, but even in these he was sincerer. When he sought pleasure, he sought it not affectedly but as a sensational reality. The argument of *Sleep and Poetry* hangs on two antitheses : the first is that implied in the title, between a passive sensuous acceptance of life, imaged as a soothing dream and a gentle slumber, and a mastery of life and all its darkness by the reasoning faculty transformed through a glowing passion into inspiration, which is, as Keats sees, the true function of poetry. He admits this, but even in his admission he realises his own present inadequacy, and looks yearningly on the life of pleasure, which against his sensuous inclination he must leave. He knows that he is " not yet a glorious denizen Of thy wide heaven," and he loves the intoxication of the earth to the point of wishing " to die a death of luxury " there. Further, he is wiser than Wordsworth or Coleridge because he understands that it is only through " All that was for our human senses fitted," and through " the events of this wide world " that a poet may in any completely courageous sense win to a realisation and expression of immortality. He is too rich in humanity and the ardours of life to wish to attain it by any other path. In the ten years in which he is to overwhelm himself in poetry his duty is to blaze out that path, and in his conviction of what that path implies, the second antithesis arises.

It is between naturalism and idealism, and is analogous to that between sleep and poetry. The animal being refining himself into a natural ecstasy has to be supplanted by one who not only reacts sensuously to nature's joyous daylight externality, but also attempts a rational interpretation of her mystery, her veiled potencies, even her horrors. The pleasure of sense native to the animal and shared with universal nature has to be transformed into the delights and pains of philosophic understanding, enriched by passion until it becomes ecstatic intuition, and by sympathy until it comprehends the misery of every human heart. He must bid unreflective, animal joys farewell:

> " Yes, I must pass them for a nobler life,
> Where I may find the agonies, the strife
> Of human hearts."

The figure by which he images such a wrestling with the problem of nature and of life is the charioteer, who

> " Looks out upon the winds with glorious fear,"

but

> " Most awfully intent
> The driver of those steeds is forward bent,
> And seems to listen: O that I might know
> All that he writes with such a hurrying glow."

He could not know, save after a long apprenticeship to life and an ardent study of her recurrent phenomena. It was all darkness and confusion, or all unanalysable sunlight. The advance of his perception lies in the fact that he recognised this wider province of life with all its possibilities of experience, and admitted the necessity of knowing. Meanwhile it was only a sense of the vast unanalysable import of life which possessed him. And in this supra-sensuous emancipation from self and fusion with the elements, a poet is apt at first to lose his bearings. Between the enlightened shore of the ultimate idea and the narrow crowded province of fact which he has abandoned, rocks a dark and capricious sea. On the tides of this sea he is now borne forward almost into sight of his goal, now tossed backward to his original starting-point. Such is Keats's condition in *Sleep and Poetry* and in much of *Endymion*. Intent on a nobler life of cambative imagination, he found

> " The visions all are fled—the car is fled
> Into the light of heaven, and in their stead
> A sense of real things comes doubly strong,
> And, like a muddy stream, would bear along
> My soul to nothingness."

It is the inevitable reaction of an idealist, not fully equipped, from a desperate effort of aspiration to the bare rock of realism. " O, I could fly With thee into the ken of heavenly powers " is an ultimate intention which the whole material world is in league to prevent. Keats's infinity of sensation was now beyond the definition of his mind, and his sense of everything approximated for a time to a sense of nothing. His intense consciousness of life identified itself with a love of death. But while the imagination might

> " Paw up against the light and do strange deeds
> Upon the clouds "

there was no basis to its activity. The bathos of
" the journey homewards to habitual self " after the
limitless intoxication of flight was only too intense,
and Keats was not yet capable of explaining the
contrast away, for his mind was still only a spectator
of his instinct's activities.   It could criticise only
before and after the event. And so in his new-found
consciousness of the infinite, he turns and makes his
famous attack on the school of poetry for whom only
the mentally defined existed,

> " a schism
> Nurtured by foppery and barbarism "

who went about beneath the decrepit standard of a
Boileau.

He knows that the acceptance by poets of any
material limits short of human life and human consciousness should be unthinkable.   Those " times
of woe " are passed, and yet the problem of human
pain and sorrow, no less than the infinite mystery of
nature, remains to be solved. Poetry is power and
light, and how should it feed upon " the burrs and
thorns of life ? " For a moment the conviction of
his new purpose fails. The joy inherent in all true
beauty cannot surrender to the ugly fact of pain;
and yet Keats does not understand the nature of
that joy wholly. Joy can only resolve pain by under-

standing it, by transforming it where it is possible
from a terrible quixotic fact into a rational idea of
which the causes are made apparent. When Keats
cries

> " And they shall be accounted poet-kings
> Who simply tell the most heart-easing things "

he has abandoned momentarily a struggle after
comprehension for which he was not yet prepared.
And though he knows not

> " The shiftings of the mighty winds that blow
> Hither and thither all the changing thoughts
> Of man ; though no great ministering reason sorts
> Out the dark mysteries of human souls
> To clear conceiving : yet there ever rolls
> A vast idea before me, and I glean
> Therefrom my liberty."

It is a dangerous liberty, liable at any moment because of its wide ambiguity to degenerate into
licence. That wilderness of unconsciousness has to
be explored by the consciousness. Well may he cry,
Ah! what a task! and seek relief in the humbler
thoughts of human morality and human pleasures

> " of brotherhood,
> And friendliness, the nurse of mutual good,"

and of precious books and sweet airs and all the
elegancies of nature. So the poem ends. Keats has
defined his aim only to the extent of discovering it
to be infinite, has embraced an ideal which he has

not the means as yet either wholly to comprehend or clothe in appropriate matter. Yet not only has his sensuousness mounted from mere material enjoyment to a point now honestly full in " the speculation of the stars," but his love of both nature and man, though still little more than a generous sentiment of sympathy, has lost almost all its early affectation. It no longer represents a pleasant emotion to be selfishly enjoyed.

iii

The infinite idea which Keats had apprehended in *Sleep and Poetry* and, attacking by direct assault, had failed to formulate, he attempted to bring into the region of consciousness by a method of allegorical image in *Endymion*. The myth itself is not of deep importance : it was borrowed because externally it offered a concrete and familiar embodiment of the antithesis which Keats was trying to resolve, namely the marriage of heaven and earth, of the idea and the fact. The poem's significance, however, is independent of the myth's traditional structure and is to be found in the imagery and symbolism which Keats himself evolved in the more fanciful than imaginative effort of rebuilding inside of it four involved and highly decorated chambers, each one represented by a book of the poem. We must allow also for the fact that in his luxurious love of adornment for its own sake, Keats tended to

obscure the significance both of his structure and of
that part of his decoration which has a symbolical
intention.*   Nevertheless, the general metaphysical
argument is distinct enough, if we do not allow our
intelligence to be clouded by the mere sensuous
pleasure to be gained often enough from passages of
rich verbal and descriptive beauty.   Keats's own
experience of life was often inadequate, as we shall
show, for his task, and it was therefore inevitable
that much creative energy which should have contributed to a struggle with his material in the interests
of imaginative truth, expended itself on the pleasure
(which is also our pleasure) of luxurious fancifulness.

The symbol of all things desired ideally—the "vast
idea" of *Sleep and Poetry*—is here the Moon,
referred to, as we have already stated, with much
descriptive beauty but no interpretative intention in
I stood Tiptoe upon a Little Hill.

Keats has thus particularised the infinite idea, in
all its beckoning mystery, to the extent of imagining
it in an object which the senses can comprehend.
The vague mystical ambition, the intuition of some
universal truth, to which his sensuousness had
brought him in a perfectly logical development, was
thus given a more direct and concrete form.   And

*Compare Letter xx.
' As to what you say about my being a Poet, I can return no
Answer but by saying that the high Idea I have of poetical fame
makes me think I see it towering too high above me. At any
rate, I have no right to talk until Endymion is finished, it will
be a test, a trial of my powers of Imagination, *and chiefly of my
invention* . . . . '

the particularisation continues.   The Moon which represents a synthesis of all things loved is only the ideal symbol at the back of the poem.   At first remove the ideal becomes Cynthia, the Moon goddess, a being nearer to human comprehension and human needs.   She personifies ideal love in a particular sense as well as in a universal.   Keats's problem, as that of all poets, was to particularise the universal; and allowing the Moon to haunt the background with her ethereal rays, he embodies love's divine principle, more nearly related to earth, in Cynthia, who combines the human and the supernatural, and in doing so he narrows his ideal of love from that which embraces all humanity as an abstract inspiration to that which ennobles or degrades the relationship of two individuals, man and woman.   The man is of course Endymion, and it is of his search for ideal love that the poem tells.   The third image is the Indian Lady, who personifies the sensuous element in love, necessary to complete and enrich what would otherwise be only an ideal abstraction.   Her significance is however for long misapprehended by Endymion, who fears that in his love for her he is proving false to the ideal, which Cynthia, and beyond her the abstract principle of the Moon, represent.   The poem ends by his discovering that the two objects of his passion are in truth one, that the ideal and the real supplement each other; but the discovery, as we shall see, by no means implies that Keats himself found the way of reconciliation.

The same antithesis therefore which we have
noticed in *Sleep and Poetry* between Naturalism
and Idealism recurs in *Endymion,* but with the
difference that Keats has now greatly defined and
particularised an idealism which was previously only
a vast intuition. That materialising process went
on doubtless in the writing of the poem, in the continual demands it made on him for concreteness, and
not only did it bring a vast new tract of unconsciousness into the conscious daylight of the mind, but it
forced on him, as on us, a realisation of the inadequacy of his own experience to supply his imagination with the material which it needed to work
upon and from which alone he could abstract and
image truth.

iv

A brief study of the poem may reveal this. The
staging of the first book is the Earth, and it opens
significantly with an appraisement of beauty, which,
if " a joy for ever," is also " a sleep full of sweet
dreams," a drowsy enchantment, more than a vital
experience. There follows the description of Latmos,
and the festival of Pan, an ecstatic spectacle of
naturalism in which finally Endymion loses his senses
and is taken to her bower by Peona, the embodiment
of natural unenquiring womanhood. Sleep, the
" comfortable bird, That broodest o'er the troubled
sea of the mind," is again invoked, but Endymion,
after being calmed, tells Peona of the vision of an

unknown goddess, dreamt of by him in a sleep within
a sleep.

> " Endymion, how strange ;
> Dream within dream ! "

and after the vision

> " Why did I dream that sleep o'erpower'd me
> In midst of all this heaven ? Why not see
> Far off, the shadows of his pionions dark,
> And stare them from me ? But no, like a spark
> That needs must die, although its little beam
> Reflects upon a diamond, my sweet dream
> Fell into nothing—into stupid sleep."

The vision haunts him, only however to disappoint
with its intangibility, and he consoles himself with
the thought of what comfort Time may bring and
his sister Peona can give.

So far then his apprehension of love might seem
to be a malady, a fever and a dream, such a passion
as Blake would have attributed to the sleepy goddess " Vala," rather than to the divine Cynthia, a
misty emanation from the earth herself. But when
Peona rallies him for yielding his manhood to such
a Circean, or rather Morphean, charm, crying :

> " Endymion !
> Be rather in the trumpet's mouth—anon
> Among the winds at large,"

and questioning

> " Why pierce high-fronted heaven to the quick
> For nothing but a dream ? "

Endymion is moved both to shame and ruth, and breaks out into his great summary of the meaning of Love. It is an exact description of Keats's own conception at this time and of the difficulties which prevented its realisation.

" Peona! ever have I long'd to slake
My thirst for the world's praises : nothing base,
No merely slumberous phantasm, could unlace
The stubborn canvas for my voyage prepar'd—
Though now 'tis tatter'd ; leaving my bark bar'd
And sullenly drifting : yet my higher hope
Is of too wide, too rainbow-large a scope,
To fret at myriads of earthly wrecks.
Wherein lies happiness? In that which becks
Our ready minds to fellowship divine,
A fellowship with essence ; till we shine,
Full alchemiz'd, and free of space. Behold
The clear religion of heaven! "

He then describes the melodious charm of music, as it can creep upon the senses in divine liquefaction, and continues :

" Feel we these things? that moment have we stept
Into a sort of oneness, and our state
Is like a floating spirit's. But there are
Richer entanglements, enthralments far
More self-destroying, leading, by degrees,
To the chief intensity : the crown of these
Is made of love and friendship, and sits high
Upon the fore-head of humanity.
All its more ponderous and bulky worth
Is friendship, whence there ever issues forth
A steady splendour, but at the tiptop,
There hangs by unseen film, an orbéd drop

> Of light, and that is love: its influence,
> Thrown in our eyes, genders a novel sense,
> At which we start and fret; till in the end
> Melting into its radiance, we blend,
> Mingle, and so become a part of it—
> Nor with aught else can our souls interknit
> So wingédly."

Up to this point the development from the accidental values of sensation to the essential insight of pure passion is manifest and logical enough. And we might conceive that Keats really understood what this ultimate passion implied, did he not almost immediately contradict it. His conception in short lacks the reason to make it consistently ideal, and immediately we find it lapses into self-indulgent luxury. Endymion continues:

> " Aye, so delicious is the unsating food,
> That men, who might have tower'd in the van
> Of all the congregated world, to fan
> And winnow from the coming step of time
> All chaff of custom, wipe away all slime
> Left by men-slugs and human serpentry,
> Have been content to let occasion die,
> Whilst they did sleep in love's elysium.
> And, truly, I would rather be struck dumb
> Than speak against this ardent listlessness."

Love then here is not an ultimate consciousness of all things, an ecstatic vibration in sympathy with the universal and harmonious elements of life, but a sleep, and a listlessness.

KEATS

The sensuous aspect was still the only one Keats really understood; he could enlarge it to its utmost possibilities of expansion; he could not yet add to it the strength and resolution of reason. Yet against this surrender to ravishment he can at least rebel. For later Endymion says:

" Now, if this earthly love has power to make
Men's being mortal, immortal; to shake
Ambition from their memories, and brim
Their measure of content; what merest whim
Seems all this poor endeavour after fame,
To one, who keeps within his steadfast aim
A love immortal, an immortal too.
Look not so wilder'd; for these things are true,
And never can be born of atomies
That buzz about our slumbers, like brain-flies,
Leaving us fancy-sick. No, no, I'm sure,
My restless spirit never could endure
To brood so long upon one luxury,
Unless it did, though fearfully, espy
A hope beyond the shadow of a dream."

It is no more than a fearful hope, of which only experience and knowledge can bring the confirmation, but it is enough to give Endymion " a more healthy countenance "; and, intent on meditation and determined to surrender no longer to the mere suggestiveness of nature, he " stept into the boat and launch'd from land." He has left the earth behind, but not, as we shall see, the limitations of an earth-bound consciousness alternating between extreme stimulation and soporific stupor.

In the second book of the poem, Endymion
wanders beneath the Earth, in the third beneath the
Sea. And we may say summarily that in the one
Keats is searching after the truth of Love in its
primitive aspect, as a creative essence, prior to its
materialisation on Earth; in the other for proof of
the survival of Love hereafter; that the one reflects
the origin of Life, the other the issues of Death. In
both, for lack of experience, he proves himself
imaginatively inadequate, and is often compelled to
let his fancy roam luxuriously and involvedly, for
want of any clear and beckoning idea. The underworld which Endymion visited was not such a one
as that with which we are familiar, for example, in
the works of Dostoevsky, a place of squalid lust where
creatures, in whom the distinctive human mind has
not been allowed to develop, move and function little
raised from the primitive slime. Keats's underworld
is a subterranean region fancifully created, where the
life-principle is shown to be little less beautiful, if
more limited in its activity, than it can be on earth
itself, and into which the ethereal idea of love,
imaged in Cynthia, penetrates like a star into the
depths of dark waters. Keats was at home on
earth, he was a human pulse in her creative energy,
and so he could in the first book depict earthly love
with an exact appreciation of all its sensuous
possibilities. But of the life-principles of brute

creation that lurked darkly beneath her sunny externality, he was scarcely yet competent to judge, nor of that mystery which seemed to contradict nature's process—the possible survival of the human soul after death. And therefore the second book of the poem, and to a less degree the third, in both matter and imagery, are too little distinguished from the first. They are merely an attempt on Keats's part to develop his consciousness of human love, and so of the ideal which such love embodies, however imperfectly, by associating with traditionally tragic or frustrated lovers in a world of fanciful mystery. This association certainly does serve to conduct Endymion from a fanciful to an actual sensuousness, from a listless sentimentalism to a state of honest desire, and prepares him for the acceptance of the Indian Lady in the last book, and so for the final reconciliation of the real with the ideal: but Keats himself, as we can plainly see from the language of the poem, does not in either of these two books advance his perception of either sensuous or ideal love far beyond the point which he had already reached.

The second book opens with a typical expression of preference for weak and rather enervated amorousness over heroism,

> " Juliet leaning
> Amid her window-flowers—sighing—weaning
> Tenderly her fancy from its maiden snow,
>   . . . . the silver flow

> Of Hero's tears, the swoon of Imogen,
> Fair Pastorella in the bandit's den,
> Are things to brood on with more ardency
> Than the deathday of empires."

The fact to notice here is not the distaste for martial
activity, which to a poet is reasonable enough, but
the quality of the love preferred, and the examples
chosen. " Sighing, swooning, brooding " are proof
enough that the sensuous quality persists. Endymion's attention however is attracted by a golden
butterfly,
> " upon whose wings
> There must be surely character'd strange things,"

and by its airy motion, felicitously described, and
symbolical surely of visionary perception, is roused
from his langour, and led to a nymph. In her cool
beauty " uprisen to the breast, In the fountain's
pebbly margin," she represents, we suppose, the
pure spring of life, unsullied as yet by any association with the matter of earth. She sympathises
with the bitterness of his love and his care, but she
realises the inadequacy of her own innocence to
explain the truth of things. For

> " Woe is me. I am but as a child
> To gladden thee : "

and
> " thou must wander far
> In other regions, past the scanty bar
> To mortal steps, before thou canst be ta'en
> From every wasting sigh, from every pain,
> Into the gentle bosom of thy love."

Endymion realises afresh the inadequacy of mere desire, and the awful need of effort.   He has to "keep off the burr Of smothering fancies."   For

> " This is human life : the war, the deeds,
> The disappointment, the anxiety,
> Imagination's struggles, far and nigh,
> All human ; bearing in themselves this good,
> That they are still the air, the subtle food,
> To make us feel existence, and to shew
> How quiet death is."

Here is the struggle for absolute imaginative consciousness, for that eternal inner harmony to be won only by a complete identifying of self with all things. And Keats knows only too well his present incompetence :

> " but for me,
> There is no depth to strike in."

He is ignorant of life, and so alone with self, and compelled to create by a continual self-absorption and self-consumption.   The despairing satiety involved in such a true perception of his own, or Endymion's, small grasp of truth at that moment, leads him to appeal once again to Cynthia, to his ideal image.   She answers him with

> " He ne'er is crowned
> With immortality, who fears to follow
> Where airy voices lead : so through the hollow,
> The silent mysteries of earth, descend ! "

The idea of life is to be found no less truly in the dark cavern of pain than in the wide heaven of ecstasy. Yet of those " sparry hollows of the world," it must be confessed that Keats knows little. He finds the region to be " one faint eternal eventide of gems," a neutral void starred with strange crystals. It may be that such an underworld is

> " past the wit
> Of any spirit to tell, but one of those
> Who, when this planet's sphering time doth close,
> Will be its high remembrancers."

A condition of protoplasm is of its nature undefined, is behind the possibility of reason, and where Keats seems to us most imaginatively true in his description, is in his emphasis of the silence, and the emptiness, and the solitude, as of one imprisoned in a grey and hateful vacuum. It is after all the only form which mind could draw out of a condition of unconsciousness, and we feel that he is most false when he allows his fancy to impose on such a state, brilliant and even definite adornment. He is indeed then "tracing fantastic figures with his spear." And from this confusion of vagueness and precision he appeals once more to Cynthia, named here possibly with a subtle difference of meaning, Diana. The immortal idea exists as a germ, even in the chaotic original substance of earth, but that it should be figured so materially as in a goddess, honoured with a temple, seems exaggerated and inappropriate. Endymion, like his creator, longs to escape from his perplexity into the breath of Heaven and the freedom of the idea as it reveals itself in the beauty of the earth. He cries :

" O, think how I should love a bed of flowers !—
Young goddess! let me see my native bowers !
Deliver me from this rapacious deep ! "

He is not delivered. " The obstinate silence came heavily again," but over the marble floor of the temple the desired flowers spring up, to be followed by the faint charm of sleepy music. The very conditions which he should have left behind him when he deserted the earth persist in the underworld. The inanity itself is vanished and there is neither pain nor confusion, but all the elegances of a pagan civilisation, and we feel that in admitting this, Keats was admitting a failure to understand the secrets of being, or the nature of the place to which he had conducted Endymion. Once again the music tortures Endymion, appealing first with heavenly suggestiveness, then sickening with hellish satiety, then vanishing in elemental passion—the three qualities of sensuousness reiterated. He regains, however, his sense of pleasure when he comes to a pleasant myrtle wood, and thence to a chamber, where he discovers Adonis sleeping on a " silken couch of rosy pride," and guarded by Cupids. The scene is such as we should associate with Paradise rather than with the underworld, and in so far as Keats is depicting

a pagan Paradise, a place where only sensuous
beauty exists at its most perfect, and untroubled as
on earth by questionings of reason, he is possibly
justified in placing it beneath the earth. Yet we still
hold that while a condition of exquisite sensuousness
may in all truth be located on the earth, as representing a state of nature at its richest and most
refined, the underworld is unsuited for staging such
a scene, being a region where life-energies are too
rude for refinement, and too chaotic to be truly represented by a spectacle of languid and luxurious
beauty. It should be too vitally formless to be a
place of refinement, even if it lack the cheerless in-
scription that guarded Dante's " Hell." But Keats
was as yet incapable of imagining horror, pain,
brutality, or nature in her crudity or elemental
callousness. And his underworld quickly develops
once again into a region of fanciful sensuousness, in
which actuality is lost in a mist of sentiment.
Adonis himself describes it as immortal. It is a
place where the fruit of life is ever at perfect bloom,
and age and decay are unknown. It has all the
sentimental aspect of Rousseau's " state of nature,"
which was in fact " nasty, brutish and mean." But
its condition is, as ever in Keats's conception of
sensuousness, one of amorous sleep ; in which activity
is but a dream. The love of Adonis with its " em-
bracements warm " as Venus tells, is a fever, if an
immortal one. It is kin to that of Endymion himself,
whose " days are wild with love," who tastes in his

exotic passion the poison of misery. It is difficult
to determine what quality of love Venus embodies,
or whether Keats himself had any clear idea of it.
She encourages Endymion with the statement that
one day he will be blest, which makes it appear as if
she represented more than the sensuousness implied
in her relationship with Adonis. It is possible that
like Cynthia, she embodies confusedly the divine
ideal. Endymion, passing along a diamond balustrade (a gaudy and rather vulgar adornment even
for a pagan Paradise!), comes upon Mother Cybele.
She doubtless represents the creative principle of life,
but except that the vision of her rouses him to cast
off his " mental slough," perhaps in the realisation
of the positive activity for which she stands, her
attributes other than majesty are not defined. The
balustrade then without explanation breaks off in
middle air. All such pieces of arbitrary stage-
managing almost invariably signify that Keats's
mind and fancy have come to a cul de sac, which
compels him to find some new point of departure.
An eagle in this case bears Endymion off to a jasmine
bower, " all bestrown with golden moss," and with
that marvellous resilience of appetite common to
pagan Paradises

> " his every sense had grown
> Ethereal for pleasure."

Yet the " dewy luxury " once again palls. He is

> " So sad, so melancholy, so bereft!
> Yet still I feel immortal! "

And once again inevitably he appeals to Cynthia,
to the ideal which, amid the exuberant vegetation of
his sense, he can grasp at but not hold.

> " O my love,
> My breath of life, where art thou? "

It is the petition repeated once again from universal
consciousness for that eternal being in relation to
another, unattainable by the senses alone. And yet
when Cynthia comes, the supposed embodiment in
Keats's mind of this ideal intuition, it is with indolent arms that he stretches to her, with bliss that he
grasps her naked waist, with ravishment and doting
cries that they tremble to each other. There could
be no greater proof of Keats's incapacity at this time
to rise above the allurements of his senses, than this
passage in which he denies and dishonours his ideal
in almost every line, with " toying hands " and
" smooth excesses," " entwining soft embraces,"
" milky sovereignties," "slippery blisses." We cannot wonder that Endymion's temples beat to an unhealthy measure, that " tranced dulness " and
frightening lethargies threatened. As Cynthia and
Endymion " richly feast " and " taste the life of
love," they eat the forbidden fruit as surely as those
two first parents of ours in Eden. If this were an
incident symbolical of the underworld, it would be

well enough; nay, in the later passages, the very impetuous onrush of the ravishment, the alternations of perfervid ecstasy and melting langour have the rich full taste of insolent paganism, of the flesh asserting its glorious godhead. We are moved to echo Browning's words

> " Thou art shut
> Out of the heaven of spirit; glut
> Thy sense upon the world."

But what is intolerable in its falsity is that Keats should make his embodiment of ideal love a partner to the sugary squalor. We need no evidence more damning of the unreliable vagueness of his conception at this time. The only symbolical fitness we can discover is in the significant fact that when " the fair visitant at last unwound Her gentle limbs," she "left the youth asleep." Sleep and death are the two graces as they are the two gifts of nature.

Yet the purpose of this union of Endymion and Cynthia was we believe conceived aright. It is the manner which is so strangely wrong. Keats doubtless meant here to materialise Endymion's sensuous conception of love, which up to this point has been fantastic, dream-laden and without substance. But, overpowered by his appetite—a not infrequent occurrence—he debased and vulgarised his ideal figure, and made her partner to an experience unworthy of her truth, her beauty, or her dignity. It was a profound, intolerable lapse.

Endymion, we note, when he woke, " hung his

head," for loneliness, not for shame. " Love's madness he had known " ;

> " O he had swoon'd
> Drunken from pleasure's nipple " :

yet he has purged his appetite through this physical experience, and gained the material on which his mind can feed, and from which truth can come.

> " No longer did he wage
> A rough-voic'd war against the dooming stars.
> No, he had felt too much for such harsh jars."

He ceased to be violent, because his mind, however melancholy, had facts to consider. It need no longer throw itself madly against an indifferent void. And " in this cool wonder " Endymion considered his life. He passed through the whole gamut of his experience and aspirations, his early naturalism, the spur of the old bards to mighty deeds : " his plans to nurse the golden age," his wanderings up to this last ecstatic moment of bodily abandonment. He feels that now he has tasted what seems to him " the sweet soul of love " to the core, " all other depths are shallow." And then to show how deceitful and wearying and insufficient such love is, he meets in a grotto with Alpheus and Arethusa, two lovers doomed to pursue each other in an underground world, and never attain. They are the symbol of superficial passion which must always be dissatisfied; for it grasps at that which eludes the grasp and never remains constant, but ever flows faithless as a stream. Arethusa, remembering the time when she too was innocently content in the converse of earth and its breezes and its woods, complains

> " But ever since I heedlessly did lave
> In thy deceitful stream, a panting glow
> Grew strong within me; wherefore serve me so,
> And call it love? Alas, 'twas cruelty."

Endymion prays to Cynthia to make these two lovers " happy in some happy plains," and the prayer is offered equally for himself. For he, as they, has left the earth to pass underground, and is fated with them to traverse the deeps of the sea, before he reaches the liberty of the upper air. As the book ends

> " The visions of the earth were gone and fled
> He saw the giant sea above his head."

The weakness of this book lies clearly in a confusion of imagery consequent on the uncertain conception in Keats's own mind of the principle of the under-world, which he is describing. If, as suggested by some critics, it signifies as a region the element of Fire, just as the other three books do those of earth, water and air, the imagery is often as grievously inappropriate as the sense is inconsequent. For although gems and diamonds may suggest the incandescent atmosphere of such a place, the flowers, the jasmine and the myrtles, beside the music and the

silks, are incongruous decorations dictated by Keats's
desire to luxuriate in his rich descriptive powers.
But the result of this self-indulgence is far more
serious, and indeed endangers the whole fabric of the
argument, when it leads to a confusion of sensuousness and idealism, most grossly in the incident we
have cited, but not infrequently in other places
where an ideal concept of love inserts itself quite un-
consciously and fleetingly into the expression of
purely sensual passion.

vi

The third book opens with an address to the Moon;
once more the ideal is recalled, and is recognised as
pervading all the material elements. The nature of
the underworld of water is distinct from that beneath
the earth; it is, to begin with, removed a step
further from a condition of vegetation and humanity.
Death, rust, and decay predominate, and moulder-
ing scrolls and skeletons of man and mammoth strew
its floor. It fills Endymion with a cold and leaden
awe, until the sensation is dispelled by Cynthia. It
is the cavern into which all life imperfectly realised
on earth passes, whereas the other region represents
the tangled vale from which all life ascends. A moon-
beam shining on Endymion under the sea again encourages him to question what this love is that is so
potent to "teach strange journeyings." Its impulse,

he realises, is a universal curiosity which craves for
all sensations and experiences, but it is something
more.

> " What is there in thee, Moon ! that thou shouldst
>   move
> My heart so potently? when yet a child
> I oft have dried my tears when thou hast smil'd.
> Thou seem'st my sister " :

and

> " Thou wast the mountain-top—the sage's pen—
> The poet's harp—the voice of friends—the sun ;
> Thou wast the river—thou wast glory won ;
> Thou wast my clarion's blast—thou wast my steed—
> My goblet full of wine—my topmost deed :—
> Thou wast the charm of women, lovely Moon !
> O what a wild and harmonized tune
> My spirit struck from all the beautful ! "

We might think that here at last Keats has expressed
clearly through a symbol the ideality and oneness of
all things desired in their purity, that in Endymion
he has conceived at last the truth that passive sensation must share with active reason if it is to com-
pass ideal vision and ideal experience. For here wisdom, poetry, nature, noble ambition, and the charm
of wine and women are gathered under one standard,
and seem to fuse in one passionate comprehension
of ideal consciousness. But the lines which follow
prove that once more this is a sensation of truth yet
unconfirmed by the reason, and therefore unreliable.

Endymion still persists in falsely dividing the sensuous from the ideal:

" But, gentle Orb! there came a nearer bliss—
My strange love came—Felicity's abyss!
She came, and thou didst fade, and fade away
Yet not entirely: no, thy starry sway
Has been an under-passion to this hour.
Now I begin to feel thine orby power
Is coming fresh upon me: O be kind,
Keep back thine influence, and do not blind
My sovereign vision.—Dearest love, forgive
That I can think away from thee and live!
Pardon me, airy planet, that I prize
One thought beyond thine argent luxuries!
How far beyond! "

This is indeed a dilemma of involved self-contradiction! The memory of that "nearer bliss" enjoyed in the underworld interposes between him and his ideal desire. He has a dim intuition that " Felicity's abyss," though more imminent and potent in its attractiveness, is inferior to the "orby power " which is renewing its influence over him. Yet he is loth that this influence should prevail lest it should blind his " sovereign vision," proof enough that he misconceives its quality, since the ideal only clears the vision. He apologises in turn to Cynthia and the Moon for an apparent infidelity to each. It is the inevitable distraction consequent on the artificial divorce of two parts of an unity which supplement each other: and just as he recognises in his sensuous

experience an " under-passion " of idealism, so in his
address to the " airy planet " he intrudes a description which is weakly sensuous—" thine argent
luxuries." Endymion (and Keats) has here therefore ceased to find idealism and sensuousness abso-
lutely opposed, but he has only reached the point of
commingling instead of combining them and thereby
destroys the reality or efficacy of either. His state
is immediately illustrated by his meeting with
Glaucus and Scylla which follows.

Glaucus, in his relationship with Scylla and Circe,
is an example of the confusion of ideal and sensuous
love. And he is paying the penalty for it in this
underworld of death, until his consciousness limited
by the bonds of sense, which cannot resolve the
secret of death and so restore him to life, is re-
deemed by one who comes with ideal knowledge
from outside. Such a being Glaucus recognises
Endymion to be.

> " thou openest
> The prison gates that have so long opprest
> My weary watching."

And he is such a being, not because he has attained
to ideal knowledge, but because he has " lov'd an unknown power "—the " known unknown " in fact
which Endymion implored in Cynthia's arms. Glaucus
tells his story, which is almost identical with Endymion's. He lived at first in happy and lonely enjoyment of instinct in the upper world of nature.

> " But the crown
> Of all my life was utmost quietude:
> There did I love to lie in cavern rude,
> Keeping in wait whole days for Neptune's voice,
> And if it came at last, hark, and rejoice! "

We notice the early passivity of his enjoyment. It was followed by distempered longings, the result of pleasurable satiety, and he plunged into the deep waters, he " interknit his senses " with the material which he had previously drawn into himself from without, and intimately shared the ebb and flow of organic life, and thought it freedom. Then he fell in love with Scylla.

> " I lov'd her to the very white of truth,
> And she would not conceive it."

Scylla presumably symbolises ideal desire, and her reason for rejecting Glaucus' love is to be imputed to its inedaquacy, as representing only complete instinctive passion. It is because of this that he falls under the spell of Circe, " this arbitrary queen of sense," whom he is unable to resist. The remembrance of Scylla only remains as a faint " underpassion," as that of the moon did when Endymion lay in Cynthia's arms. But eventually he discovers Circe as the deathly deformity which she really is. He too longs to be delivered

> " from this cumbrous flesh
> From this gross, detestable, filthy mesh."

But Circe's power is so great that it can even condemn to ugliness, disablement and age one who has
" thews immortal " and is of a " heavenly race."
He returned to the deeps only to find Scylla cold and
dead.   There, however, he is given a scroll of strange
and deep significance, of the writing upon which this
is the most important passage :

> " Yet he shall not die,
> These things accomplish'd—If he utterly
> Scans all the depths of magic, and expounds
> The meaning of all motions, shapes and sounds,
> If he explores all forms and substances
> Straight homeward to their symbol essences,
> He shall not die.   Moreover, and in chief,
> He must pursue this task of joy and grief
> Most piously—all lovers tempest-tost,
> And in the savage overwhelming lost,
> He shall deposit side by side, until
> Time's creeping shall the dreary space fulfil :
> Which done, and all these labours ripened,
> A youth by heavenly powers lov'd and led
> Shall stand before him, whom he shall direct
> How to consummate all.   The youth elect
> Must do the thing, or both will be destroyed."

This represents the very summit of understanding to
which Keats has been climbing, and yet he is plainly
unaware of the heights he has scaled.   Well may he
cry with Endymion :

> " We are twin brothers in this destiny."

For the first time he has defined here without one
false word his intuition of ideal desire.   It entails,

in place of an acceptance of motions, shapes and
sounds, forms and substances, a penetrating understanding of them, a realisation of their symbolical,
not their material, meaning: of their essence, not
their appearance. This is to be attained only by a
complete comprehension of them, in which the rational
perception has to ally itself with sensuous sympathy.
By the depths of magic, Keats must imply the secrets
of life and death, both of which can only be learnt by
one in conscious communion with perfect beauty, and
aware therefore of what is essential and what inessen-
tial to the purest embodiment of life in any material
form. The false magic is that of exaggerated sense,
of destructive allurement, which stifles life through
persuading it to absorb matter undiscriminatingly,
exercising no selection over it in the interests of harmony, but accepting everything that gratifies in the
moment; the true magic is that of spirit, of creative
energy in which the mind controls the instinct to
accept only such matter as will contribute to a vital
organism expressing its vitality in the harmonious
fusion of each active element. Pursuing the " task
of joy and grief," which is the other labour imposed
upon him, is only an application of this active seer-
ship to human life. As the poet must study nature
with a complete consciousness of all her elements and
their particular values, so he must take upon his
shoulders the burden of humanity, and discover in
the world of men the essences beneath every form.
To this latter task Keats was to return with more

urgency in *Hyperion*; but the problem of both humanity and nature which he saluted sentimentally in his first poem is here rationally accepted, and if not solved, the right manner of solving it is discovered and stated.

Keats probably, no more than Endymion, understood the complete significance of these cryptic words. He had seized upon the truth, as a poet must, immediately. His dissatisfaction with naturalism had swelled up to a passionate protest, a passionate demand for knowledge, only to sink back again baffled. In the person of Endymion and by rational proclamation he was enabled to free Glaucus and many a wasting lover. But he had certainly not freed himself. " The pure wine of happiness," which the delivered tasted, " from fairy-press ooz'd out," has something of poison in its honey-sweet. The Neptune's hall into which they flocked, the luxurious encouragement of Venus, suggest that Enchantment has once again grown drunken. And if this be fitting for an underworld lush and Pagan, the scroll with its ideal argument seems as inappropriate to it as Cynthia was in her amorous profuseness in the previous book. Indeed both of these books present a tangled confusion of metaphysic, and an arbitrary choice of imagery which fancy, not imagination, dictates. There is a sameness too about both of them which proves that Keats in his uncertain vision of the springs of life and the wells of death, merged the one into the other. After the first passage descriptive of the watery world Keats seems to have abandoned any attempt to portray a region of death, save in the rigid spectacle of gaunt, quiescent sensualism, which Glaucus personifies, and even he is served by sea-nymphs in "beauteous vassalage," while after his deliverance all the exuberance of a wildly natural world buds out afresh to clothe a place which we expect to symbolise only the decay of life lived materially. For Death is the limited conception of the senses which view life not as an essence expressing itself through different degrees of reality in varying forms, but as matter ultimate in itself and significant of nought else. A sensuous love is therefore death; for it is the attraction of matter to matter. This the doomed Glaucus may well symbolise, but his deliverance is artificial. The scroll encourages us to hope for a true deliverance, but words do not work a miracle. Glaucus delivered amid delicious symphonies is as dead to an ideal conception as he was before. Only the words tell us that

"Death fell a-weeping in his charnel-house."

Further, the sensuous experience of love in the two underworlds of fire and water is embodied in incidents too similar in character. Alpheus and Arethusa, Glaucus and Scylla, are distinct in this, that the enslavement of the first is to perpetual movement, the condition of natural life; and of the second to decrepitude and rigidity; but the conversation of the four is bafflingly alike, and does not represent clearly enough the distinction that does exist between sensuousness which is the lust of life, seeking permanence by perpetual activity, and that which, having tasted satiety, searches in vain and rigid despondency for a passion which will not destroy its possessor. Sensuous life and sensuous death mingle together in each of the underworlds, and with them ideal desire, now visioned in its true sovereignty, now prostituted to the level of the servile place.

The truth is that Keats was in process of defining his instinctive perceptions. In these two books, impulsive emotion, self-created in the act of writing, constantly blurred his vision, and although they contain true definitions of both ideal and physical desire, the two types are more frequently to be found falsely mingled in opposition to each other, instead of positively fused.

vii

In the last book of the poem Endymion is removed to the air. He finds a fair Indian maid, who signifies again sensuous passion.

> " there she lay
> Sweet as a musk-rose upon new-made hay ;
> With all her limbs on tremble, and her eyes
> Shut softly up alive."

His protestations of passion are of a like enervated quality :

> " Dear maid, sith
Thou art my executioner, and I feel
Loving and hatred, misery and weal,
Will in a few short hours be nothing to me,
And all my story that much passion slew me ;
Do smile upon the evening of my days :
And, for my tortur'd brain begins to craze,
Be thou my nurse : and let me understand
How dying I shall kiss that lilly hand."

She sings the lovely dirge to sorrow, and the glorious saluatation of Bacchus, and Endymion is enthralled as by a Siren. He wishes even to "sip her tears," and they ride together in the air on winged horses, seeing Sleep, the recurrent symbol of passivity, journeying beneath them, until they too fall beneath his spell. Endymion dreams luxuriously of Pagan vintages and of the earthly seasons, and lastly of Cynthia coming to him in the form of the moon. But in the act of springing towards her he awakes, and is torn between the desire of the beckoning Moon and of " the panting side of his delicious lady." He kisses her, and the shadow of Cynthia melts away, leaving him in desperation, exclaiming :

> " Is there nought for me,
Upon the bourne of bliss but misery ? "

His desire is indeed " joy gone mad, with sorrow cloy'd," because it is " pillow'd in lovely idleness," and as

> " The moon put forth a little diamond peak,
> No bigger than an unobserved star,
> Or tiny point of fairy scimitar ;
> Bright signal that she only stoop'd to tie
> Her silver sandals, ere deliciously
> She bow'd into the heavens her timid head,"

the Indian maid fades away in the " cold moon-shine," and Endymion is left in the cave of passive Despair. This is nobly described, and is in its comprehension of all pain as free from the insults and petty agonies of space as Paradise, in its comprehension of all bliss. It is the native hell of utter disillusionment.

> " But few have ever felt how calm and well
> Sleep may be had in that deep den of all.
> There anguish does not sting : nor pleasures pall :
> No hurricanes beat ever at the gate,
> Yet all is still within and desolate,"

with which we may compare

> " The island-valley of Avilion,
> Where falls not hail, or rain, or any snow,
> Nor ever wind blows loudly."

Endymion has passed for the last time through the three stages decreed to the baffled idealist surrendering to the sensuous, the stages of physical ecstasy, fevered sleep, and waking disquietude. And in an utter realisation of the helplessness of that " grievous feud " which separates the reasoning and the instinctive faculties, he has won to a consciousness of nothingness, which is the end decreed to sensuous experience, as universal comprehension is to super-rational or spiritual. He is in the pit beneath good and evil, instead of on the heights above it. The senses, exercised alone, in the end annihilate the ego, and Endymion has found content because he has lost human consciousness, and so ceased from effort. He has " no self-passion or identity." The darkness and stillness of the place are that of universal liquefaction, into which all matter has melted as the last glimmer of a constructive idea faded from it.

Endymion is however borne from the cavern to Latmos, and there again finds the Indian lady and is filled, true to the quenchless ebullience of Nature, with all his old weakly raptures.

> " My Indian bliss !
> My river-lily bud ! one human kiss !
> One sigh of real breath—one gentle squeeze,
> Warm as a dove's nest among summer trees,
> And warm with dew at ooze from living blood."

That there should be no change in the quality of his love is surely a grievous error. That sense should sink into a passive nonentity, hugely impressive, only to turn again on a rebound of erotic voluptuousness to a natural world, is to destroy something of the purpose or significance of Endymion's wandering. It is true that much against his will he rejects the pleasure he desires,

" There never liv'd a mortal man who bent
His appetite beyond his natural sphere,
But starv'd and died."

and

" we might commit
Ourselves at once to vengeance; we might die;
We might embrace and die: voluptuous thought!
Enlarge not to my hunger, or I'm caught
In trammels of perverse deliciousness.
No, no, that shall not be: thee will I bless
And bid a long adieu."

But his appetite is in no way purged; the sight of
the Indian maid only restores its vigour, and redeems
his life " from too thin breathing." His wanderings
have only served to materialise his sensuousness and
reveal to him its peril. He bows himself to Chastity
and Cynthia's service, and accepts Peona as his only
associate: and then suddenly, " by some unlook'd
for change," in the short space of twenty lines, the
sensuous image is spiritualised. The Indian maid is
metamorphosed. She appears as Cynthia, and all,
we are told, is well.

Endymion kneels down before his goddess " in a
blissful swoon." It matters not that no single word
shows him to be changed in heart or mind from the
voluptuous lover of the moment before, his love is
sanctified by a trick of allegory, and the soul and the
body are compelled into reconciliation. Well might
Peona go home " through the gloomy wood in won-

derment." For she had been deceived by a device too apparent to convince even a simpleton.

Keats, at this point in his development, could not have ended it otherwise. The whole poem proves that just as in his first volume he had accepted nature for the most part externally, weaving fancies about her, while her idea remained something bodiless and unexplainable, so here he has only advanced to the point where he can speak intimately the language of human instinct, expressing nature from within in language rich and excessive as her own vegetation; but that a true consciousness of her idea still escapes him, in the confusion of matter which repeatedly overwhelmed his senses. For moments he seems to have perceived what the idea was by purely intellectual judgment, as in the words written on the scroll. But such comprehension was unreliable; it represented a mental abstraction divorced from sensual experience, and as soon as the invitation to sensuousness returned, the idea was lost, and influenced his estimation of sensuous pleasure not at all. In short, his apprehension of the idea of life is at this point as external as his former perception of nature. And so even his principal images, the Moon, Cynthia, the Indian maid, are not pure symbols of ideal, intellectual, or sensuous beauty; they are confused and changeable allegories, and, apart from their merely arbitrary reconciliation at the end, have been too vaguely indistinguishable throughout the course of the poem to reveal any new significance in their union.

The language of the poem bears testimony to the same lack of balance in Keats's creative condition. Passive assimilation and absorption preponderate over active originality; the reason strives desperately to hew a way through its entanglements, and although it reduces thicket after thicket to perfect and lovely order, it leaves many overgrown with tropical undergrowth, while in the very necessity of cutting a path through the thicket in front, Keats loses sight of either purpose or direction.

A poet's reason should function in two ways: it should conceive ideas of absolute truth from the matter of life, and it should re-express these ideas at their purest and most intense through the medium of language and the mastery of image. The image is only true in so far as it answers to the idea and to the emotion by which the poet was enabled to grasp the idea. In this it is distinct from such images as fancy creates out of a wanton appetite, which serve as a possibly pleasing, but only superficial and self-sufficient decoration, lacking all deeper significance. Keats in Endymion had attempted to express his intuition of an infinite idea through particular experience of human love. His sensuousness was yet too powerful, his reason too weak. He lapses frequently into the mere indulgence of fancy and of rich and fanciful imagery for its own sake. Yet just as Endymion's passive sentimentalism develops in the course of his wanderings into honest physical desire, so Keats's own visionary vagueness was materialised by the experience of writing this poem. The feud which existed within him between the faculties of instinct and of imagination became defined in his mind. His idealism became more a conscious effort after truth, and less an unconscious surrender to life.*

After Endymion, he contented himself for a short time with perfecting his style, that is, with increasing his mental control over an instinctive genius, on the limited level of technique. In this period he attained to the highest point of comparative accomplishment. He realised in fact completely a limited aim, and in doing so he strengthened his intelligence for the coming contest, when he should accept a vaster task than that of perfecting material beauty, and harmoniously ordering sensuous images.

That task was no less than an imaginative reading of human destiny; it comprised a renewed assault on that " vast idea " which he had visioned to himself in the formless void. We shall see that death only cast him down, when he had his foot on the citadel.

viii

Keats's *Tales and Odes* have not unnaturally been admired more than any other of his poems. We have already remarked that the middle and late XIXth

* Compare Letter xxxiv.

Of Endymion Keats writes :—' The whole thing must, I think, have appeared to you, who are a consecutive man, as a thing almost of mere words, but I assure you that, when I wrote it, it was a *regular stepping of the Imagination towards a truth.*'

century preferred art which appealed to a luxurious appetite, rather than that which by the force and amplitude of its vision demanded imaginative effort. To such taste Keats's middle period must always offer an ideal harvest. For no poet has ever pressed purer or richer juice out of the grapes of sensation, or poured it into a more perfect chalice, than he did at this stage of his development. At the same time no poet can ever have been so self-aware of the limitations to which he was momentarily submitting.

A letter recently published by Miss Amy Lowell shows with what a ruthless sense of values he dismissed *Lamia* and *The Eve of St. Agnes* to the haunts of prettiness and sentimentality. And so far as matter, distinct from form, goes, he was right. They are sentimental because they lack a constructive idea, or play to perfection with a superficial one.

It is clear from the development in the style of the language that Keats was at this time consciously aiming at self-discipline rather than new or profounder self-assertion. He had attempted to capture the ideal by impetuous rushes into a dark void, only to fall back exhausted into the real, and without the energy to shape that to perfect order. His energies were thus divided between an instinctive acceptance of nature and an unanalysed perception of some idea of which both nature and man were the expression. The dual aim, he realised, denied him full accom-

E

plishment in either field, and for the moment he accepted the humbler task. If *Sleep and Poetry* is early Spring, and *Endymion* late Spring, then *Isabella* is languid June, *The Eve of St. Agnes* ripe Midsummer, *Lamia* fevered August, and the *Ode to Autumn*, the mellow, misty season of the Fall. Such a definition is indeed as accurate as it is picturesque. For in this period Keats's natural genius passed through its regular seasons; it submitted itself like Nature to the impulse of organic growth.

The hint of heaven, of ethereal presences, and symbols divine, did indeed fall on his ears with suggestive persistence during this period, and he responded to it with vague indecision in some of the *Odes*, and more directly in his labour on *Hyperion*, at the same time as his natural genius was bearing fruit in *The Eve of St. Agnes*, and again in his early labour at the revised version of *Hyperion*, (as a recently published letter proves), coincidently with the writing of *Lamia*. But the definite rejection of Nature and the pure pursuit of the ideal followed his last perfect expression of sensuous fact in the *Ode to Autumn*.

Keats's increasing mastery over his medium can be traced very clearly by anyone who studies the poems on their technical side. Up to this time he had indulged in realistic impressionism. He looked on words like a lover, he relished every tone and colour for its own sake, and like one who cannot see the vale beneath him and the far hills and the stooping sky, because each moment his eyes are captured by some lovely flower or shining leaf in the foreground, so, true to instinct, which lives in the moment and seizes that nearest to its hand regardless of all else, he seized upon a word, an image or a situation which delighted him, regardless of the perspective of the whole poem. We find therefore either speedily reduplicated images, each expressing in a different way the truth which his imagination has grasped, a method exemplified at its happiest in the famous passage " Stop and consider," and less happily in the sonnet " How many bards gild the lapses of time ? " or else passages of lush description, perfect at times in themselves, but bearing either exaggerated or little relation to the complete world of which they are supposed to be subservient parts.

Keats now applied his mind to perfecting the work of natural sensibility, to reducing a sensuous chaos to its most attractive order. The improvement in *Isabella* may not be very marked. But there are two points to be noticed. Firstly, that the poem is written in rhyming stanzas, and secondly, that it is a tale told in the person of another, and with details already mapped out by Boccaccio, its original creator. It is true that in the handling of the details Keats exercised his own discretion, and that he entered into Lorenzo's person as if it were his own, but the fact remains that in adopting both a situation and characters already created, already set imperishably in that everlasting languid summer of the Decameron, Keats was enabled to defer as it were the dilemma of his own genius. He could be a sensuous, even a sickly lover in the person of Lorenzo without calling himself in question; for so Boccaccio had decreed it. The stanza form imposed a further limit on his exuberance, as it had with such early felicity in the sonnet on Chapman's *Homer*. For mind standardises rhythm, while emotion varies it, and it is in the perfect counterpoint of these two forces that supreme art is attained. To adopt a stanza form is to accept, if only artificially, a continual mental reminder from which the senses can never escape.

Isabella is at least a complete organism; it is a languid creation of unhealthy blood, but it hangs together, and its parts balance. Its sickliness lies in its sentimentalism, in such pseudo-Romanticism as was to weaken so much of the work of the Pre-Raphaelites. The sensuousness is exotic and sickly. Lorenzo's love is a " malady," and the odour of the charnel pervades the poem with a faint repulsiveness; death is in the air, and

> " the lilies, that do paler grow
> Now they can no more hear thy glitter's tone "

are indeed those " that fester." We are inclined to ask, as Keats does, with quaint surrender of himself to the needs of the tale,

> " Ah, wherefore all this wormy circumstance? "

Even Keats's sensuousness, we may well believe, was temporarily exhausted by *Endymion*. Here he borrowed a frame, and wove upon it threads of faded silk. The frame we know to be not of his own construction, because the pattern he has woven upon it is too thin in places to conceal the structure. Yet it is a structure, and to that degree the poem reveals an advance upon his earlier work.

Between the conclusion of *Isabella* and the writing of *The Eve of St. Agnes*, Keats went on his walking tour in Scotland. He also met Fanny Brawne. This incident is not of immediate importance, as we can see from his letters that his passion for her did not become absorbing until later. But there is little doubt that the influence of nature in her most commanding and severe aspect, as he felt it amid the Scotch mountains, both refreshed and stimulated his sensibility, and gave new strength to his will. For on his return he undertook both *Hyperion* and *The Eve of St. Agnes*.

In *Hyperion* he made his first definite and masculine effort to hew out for himself a path of perception distinct from nature's. We shall see that his mind was still diffident and his aim uncertain, and that, his purpose becoming entangled in the apparatus he had borrowed from Milton, he surrendered temporarily his effort, and turned again to nature. We will, therefore, consider this first version of *Hyperion* in conjunction with his later revision, when we come to it.

His admiration and his subsequent abandonment of a Miltonic style are both significant: for the study of Milton at this time increased his own constructive power, and the mental faculty of which style is the index. That his appetite was once more restored almost to a healthy keenness is clear from a comparison of *Isabella* with *The Eve of St. Agnes.* The mawkishness is completely, the enervation almost gone. If there is any unhealthiness, it is that of over-ripeness, and this is due more to the too perfect economy by which the beaker is filled with every drop of sweetness that it can hold, even " with beaded bubbles winking at the brim," than to any false fever in the blood. In this poem Keats gave himself to his instinct wholly—there is no suggestion of divided energy or warring consciousness. No other aim but the creation of sensuous beauty was present; the accomplishment within those chosen boundaries was supreme. The legend he took from a brief note of Burton's, which offered him far more freedom in the shaping of the narrative than *Isabella*, but the Spenserian stanza imposed an even stricter control over his instinct. And here he covered the structure completely with a rich tapestry of words and images. There is no place where the threads run thin, or the anatomy suggests itself through the flesh. Indeed the weakness of the poem is that the weaving is generally too heavy for the structure, which we feel to be bending beneath it. In places, too, notably in the incident of the " bedesman " and the feast set out by Porphyro in Madeline's chamber, threads assert themselves which are inappropriate or of too vivid colouring for the pattern viewed as a whole to absorb. These are once again instances of Keats's momentary surrender to an instinct too pleasurable to him, and attractive in itself, to be refused in the interest of the whole poem. But the mastery of the language and so of the senses which dictated it, is almost complete. The nervous energy which squandered itself in the reckless profusion of *Endymion,* flooding up in wave upon wave of un-co-ordinated images, loosely linked together, is tuned here to make organic numbers. The poem is an organism to which almost every word contributes; it reflects the perfect art of nature, of sensations discovering their own richest forms in harmony. It has nature's exuberant vegetation, and, as nature will veil her actuality in atmosphere, so Keats casts over his the illusion of Romance. For since sense cannot, as intuition, penetrate the material of life, and draw from it a beauty significant of its truth, it is compelled to beautify or sentimentalise actuality accepted externally (and often in fact discordant) by some artificial means suggestive of unreality. Such Romantic imagery at its best conveys to us hints of an infinite world beyond human experience; it brings as near to consciousness as mortal means allow the mysterious darkness, the vast intensity of an unknown, untravelled universe, of a world beyond the radius of our minds, and the dimensions of space, elemental and provocative as the moan of wind about a house at night, and only to be realised in sudden moments of haunting apprehension.

It is this suggestion of a dim impassioned world, in which life is a purer and more intimate sensation, that pervades the merely sensuous imagery of *The Eve of St. Agnes,* and breaks through the close texture with a sudden thrill as of great distances momentarily revealed, or of a door opened and closed upon a richer world, as in that rude burst of martial music upon the stillness where the " faded moon Made a dim silver twilight "—

> " O for some drowsy Morphean amulet !
> The boisterous, midnight, festive clarion,
> The kettledrum, and far-heard clarinet,
> Affray his ears, though but in dying tone :—
> The hall door shuts again, and all the noise is gone,"

though the definite allocation of the sound here necessarily lessens its mystic suggestion ; but more particularly in

> " Hark ! 'tis an elfin storm from faery land,"

and in the suggestion of a wild unearthly antiquity conveyed in the last stanza :

> " And they are gone : ay, ages long ago,
> These lovers fled away into the storm."

This romantic suggestiveness, in which instinct takes wings and rises into the realm of pure imagination, will always remain inexplicable by the reason; for in that its whole power lies. It is a witchery of sense, which combines in one passionate moment a number of images calculated both by their sense and sound to suggest an infinite world by mingling the near and the distant, the definite and the indefinite, as in a blurred picture in which distances are confused, but which is yet distinct enough to provoke and tantalise the mind, to stimulate and leave unsatisfied the sense. It is an unconscious confusion of vivid images under the stress of powerful emotion, or as in Coleridge's *Kubla Khan,* under the artificial stimulus of a drug, and it gives to us all the definition of space, while freeing us from its limitations.

The best known example of this in Keats's poems is the " Charm'd magic casements " in the *Ode to the Nightingale.* But often elsewhere the multitude of particular images, by which the senses express their pleasure in choice tangible objects, gives way to this extreme of ecstatic indefinition, which seeks to concentrate the essence of all particular attracttions in one unanalysable combination of suggestive sound and colour.

But the concrete imagery of *The Eve of St. Agnes* is almost perfect. Each word is chosen with absolute discretion and a full recognition of relationship and values. Yet each contributes its iota of luxurious sensuousness. It was inevitable therefore that with such an abundance of material, movement should be lacking. The harmonies are rich and sonorous

and beautifully modulated, the melody is at best a
tenuous thread, the whole poem is a long perfumed
moment, in which we hear the ebb and flow of stillness. That such is the effect on us is a proof of
Keats's mastery of his early effusive sensuousness.
He loaded now " every rift with ore," but he bound
each golden link into one chain. Yet in the very process his sensuousness had lost something of its early
impetuosity and resilience. It did not dart from
pleasure to pleasure, recording each and passing on.
Rather it absorbed passively, wringing every drop of
sweetness out of an experience, and suspending his
activity, as the rhythm constantly shows, upon the
climax of desire :

> " Beyond a mortal man impassion'd far
> At these voluptuous accents, he arose,
> Ethereal, flush'd, and like a throbbing star
> Seen 'mid the sapphire heaven's deep repose :
> Into her dream he melted, as the rose
> Blendeth its odour with the violet."

There is a distinct halt in the rhythm after
" ethereal," " flush'd " and " melted " which em-
phasises and enriches the abandonment to follow. Yet
although Keats had at this time, by deliberate rejection of any other aim and by selection and artistry,
refined to a point near perfection his expression of
sensuous beauty, he realised that it was now on
syrup, rather than on honey, that he fed, and that
a continued pursuit of pure sensation, however
exquisite, could only end in stupor. From this point

onwards, therefore, we find his latent idealism more and more re-asserting itself. It is apparent in its fluctuating indecision no less in his poetry than in his love-letters, and it becomes only more urgent as his strength was encroached upon by advancing disease.

ix

If Keats's career had ended with the writing of *The Eve of St. Agnes* there would have been every excuse for posterity's acceptance of him as a poet who sought beauty for beauty's sake rather than for truth's. It was indeed out of this misconception that the cult of " art for art's sake " arose. The protagonists of that superficial creed were true heirs of all Keats's young limitations; theirs was a trivial sensuousness compared to that of their great model, and their minds were not equal to the task of comprehending his philosophy or detecting behind his material felicity the consistent impulse towards idealism. And to that extent Arnold was justified in arguing that Keats, unlike Shelley and Byron and Wordsworth, has not encouraged men to strain after new concepts or seek to understand life more essentially, or indeed to live with a more passionate nobility, but he errs when he suggests that Keats himself rested content with his own perfect contribution of plastic, sensuous beauty, or was prepared to acquiesce like a vain woman in the charms of mere appearance.* Keats was healthily averse to hurrying his development; he knew that a natural growth of powers is to be preferred to hot-house forcing, and for ourselves we can only marvel at the sanity and consistency with which he advanced step by step, while each of his rich powers found its proper place in the economy of his genius. That advance cannot be indicated more clearly than by his estimation of the nature of Beauty at different points, from the happy, thoughtless

> " A thing of beauty is a joy for ever "

in *Endymion*, through premature realisation of the need of effort :

> " For 'tis the eternal law
> That first in beauty should be first in might,"

occurring in *Hyperion*, through the scarce comprehended

> " Beauty is truth, truth beauty, that is all
> Ye know on earth, and all ye need to know,"

*See letter lxxxvi.
' I must needs feel flattered by making an impression on a set of ladies. I should be content to do so by *meretricious romance verse*, if they alone, and not men, were to judge.'
And letter xcix.
' I am three and twenty, with little knowledge and middling intellect. It is true that in the height of enthusiasm I have been cheated into some fine passages, but that is not the thing.'
And letter lxxxv.
' Hunt keeps on his old way—I am completely tired of it all. He has lately publish'd a Pocket Book called the Literary Pocket-Book—full of the most sickening stuff you can imagine.'

in the *Ode on the Grecian Urn*, or the relapse into anguished complaint of

" She dwells with beauty—beauty that must die "

in the *Ode on Melancholy*, to the profounder vision of the fall of *Hyperion*—

> " whereon there grew
> A power within me of enormous ken,
> To see as a god sees, and take the depth
> Of things as nimbly as the outward eye
> Can size and shape pervade."

Keats, as we have seen, had fought his way from an indulgent to a disciplined sensuousness. In the *Odes*, personal contemplation compelled him once more to face a wider issue. Here the beauty of Time and Eternity, of Nature and of Art, of the real and ideal, are brought into anguished contrast.

Yet the contrast is so appealing and intense just because it is between two forms of sensation, one of which takes pleasure in the moment and regrets its brief continuance, and the other aspires towards some permanent condition of beauty and joy, beyond the thieving hands of time.* But the ever present

---

* Compare letter lv.

' The difference of high sensations, with and without knowledge, appears to me this : in the latter case we are falling continually ten thousand fathoms deep and being blown up again, without wings, and with all the horror of a bare-shouldered creature—in the former case, our shoulders are fledged, and we go through the same air and space without fear.'

consciousness of the contrast is the index of Keats's progress. Beauty and pleasure are no longer so much accepted as reproached. Such a condition precedes the distinguishing of the permanent from the transient on the basis of an intellectual principle, and by the exercise of absolute reason.

We cannot attach any deep significance to the *Ode on Indolence*. It was written " when my passions are all asleep, from my having slumbered till nearly eleven, and weakened the animal fibre all over me, to a delightful sensation, about three degrees on this side of faintness." It was the creation of a mood, and might be supposed to embody a complete surrender to sensation. It is the more remarkable therefore that it betokens the purpose of his mind even in its surrender to inactivity. The three figures who pass by him are Love, Ambition and Poesy, and of these Love is fair, Ambition pale of cheek " And ever watchful with fatigued eye," and Poesy, " my demon." These are analogous to the three qualities of his genius, an instinct for natural beauty, the pursuit of Idealism, and ever-driving creative impulse. He banishes the thought of them with stimulated cynicism, but in the last stanza his true sentiment appears. He is weary of being

> " dieted with praise,
> A pet-lamb in a sentimental farce,"

by people, such as the Leigh Hunt circle, whom he knows to lack a perception of what is greatly praiseworthy, and who imagine that he too is exquisitely satisfied with what he has already attained. He bids farewell to such figures, as being but the pretty decorations of luxurious fancy, the knick-knacks of poetasters' drawing rooms, and adds

> " I yet have visions for the night,
> And for the day faint visions there is store;
> Vanish, ye Phantoms! from my idle spright,
> Into the clouds, and never more return! "

Even then, in a mood in which he might be expected to welcome such conceits, it is significant that he rejects them, for a dreary indolence perhaps, but for one haunted by visions of a new purpose.

The Odes on a Grecian Urn and to a Nightingale may be considered together, both because they were written in the same month, and for the close parellelism of their mood. In each the impermanence, the discord and the decay of man is contrasted with a state of existence which Keats visions as eternal and unalterable. In neither case is the permanence one of fact; the decoration of the urn is liable to decay or the accident of breakage: the song of the nightingale passes with the night, and the songster is certainly no more eternal than man is; for the hungry generations tread down the breed of nightingales be they born as birds or men. In both cases then, it is the idea of beauty, expressed through a work of art and a voice of nature, which he contrasts with the fact of man.

" Not to the sensual ear, but, more endear'd,
Pipe to the spirit ditties of no tone."

The " Attic shape " is within the dimensions of
space in fact, it is beyond it in the idea which it
embodies through fact; the ecstasy of the immortal
bird is in fact limited by the journeying sun; it is
by the song's essential beauty that it escapes out of
time.

" Beauty is Truth," Keats summarised it, and it
was not to the sensual ear that he spoke the word,
and yet in the very arbitrary contrast between the
mortality of man and the immortality of a perfect
song, he was judging the one on a basis of sense, and
the other as a spiritual symbol. Both odes represent
with a difference a passionate escape from the hedg-
ing facts of life into the realm of pure sensation,
which is immortal only as long as the identification
of sense with the song or the work of art lasts, but
which fades when the connection is severed.

" Fled is that music—do I wake or sleep? "

Muddy time flows back upon the clear stream. And
yet must it be so? The sensation must flee, but not
so the idea which shaped the sensation into such
immaterial beauty and gave it a moral significance,
that denied the limits of space and time, and freed
Keats from the self-absorption of his senses, making
him one with all the generations of men, and with the
transcendent spirit of life itself. For that which so
purged and sublimated his sensations was the prin-

ciple of life expressing itself through matter in triumphant harmony, a harmony so unadulaterated, so far removed from the material contingencies of discord, that it rises above the destructive law of nature into a condition of pure being.

But without the idea which was an addition of Keats's human perception to a natural fact, the nightingale's song was indeed a sensation and nothing more. The element of sentimentalism therefore lies not in Keats's idealisation of nature (for harmony is the highest lesson to be learnt by man from her), but in his realistic reference to man by way of artificial contrast, and to a world " where youth grows pale, and spectre-thin, and dies."

Pure beauty is a state of being in which all the elements of an organism are in active and absolute harmony with one another, without coercion, but they must be apprehended as such by the reason of man before they become ideal. Discord and waste are in fact truer to nature than to the world of men : the sensation of perfect song is even briefer than the sensation of perfect youth, but the power of apprehending harmony and of living in conscious intimacy with it belcngs to a man's reason alone. The sensation may pass, the grey hairs may fall, but the truth of life and so the joy remains, and he who lives through every sensation does not die with the last of them, which is death itself. But he who accepts the sensation as a fact, realises the loss of the fact; to such a one

F

" But to think is to be full of sorrow
And leaden-eyed despairs,
Where Beauty cannot keep her lustrous eyes,
Or new love pine at them beyond to-morrow."

For he thinks of life only externally, and his sensation is but a moment's plunge into her calm depths, from which he returns to the fretful surface dissatisfied.

To the idealist however each sensation is but one more note in an eternal melody; he only confirms physically through his senses what he conceives rationally through his mind, namely, the absolute principle of beauty which we have just enunciated.

The physical moment passes, but the conception which it materialised remains, to figure itself subsequently in a new sensation. Thus earth becomes the medium through which man visualises a heavenly logic. He ceases to accept her only as a material body of which he is also a part. Keats, in the *Ode to the Nightingale,* sank back into the earth from which he came : his ecstasy was that of physical identity with organic life; he abandoned his humanity in disgust with its limitations,

" Now more than ever seems it rich to die."

His sense of everything approximated to a sense of nothing. It made him in love with death, with the material law of nature to which he had with his senses surrendered his mind. Because the song and the season were perfect and his sensibility was very rare, he had only to surrender himself to life to taste an ideal truth, but he was still incapable of idealising a world of men which, in its external " fever and fret," alienated his senses.   He could apprehend truth through pleasure, he could not detect it behind pain or apparent ugliness.   But the great poet has not truly realised himself until he can see heaven in the abysm of hell itself.

Both the emotional ecstasy of the Nightingale Ode and its emotional despair are the direct outcome of intense self-absorption.   Keats could not here escape the selfish hunger of his own senses, crying out for more and more loveliness with a greed that seizes on Beauty as a transitory luxury, significant only in fact, to be consumed with transcendent relish, and to be regretted as a sumptuous banquet passed.   It is a very material apprehension, ideal only in its expression.

That which inspired the *Ode on a Grecian Urn* was the memory of perfect sculpture, not of Nature's voice.   It was the beauty of man's creation, not of earth's.   And the result therefore was more of an approach to considered philosophy and less instinctive abandonment, more consolation and less despair. It is of little matter that " Old age shall this generation waste " for " Beauty is truth " and shall survive the ages.   Such a philosophy is indeed imperfect if it allow the eternal idea of beauty to a work of art and refuse it to man, of whose spirit every perfect work of art is the expression: but Keats has laid his hand, if tentatively, upon a principle, by which life as well as art comes to have a reason, and is not merely an accepted sensation. In wedding beauty with truth he consciously related sensuousness to idealism, and in hailing the permanence of art above that of nature, he affirmed, however tentatively, that it is the duty of human reason to induce order in the confusion of life by control and selection.

This principle he could as yet apply only to the materials of his art; he had not, as the poems that follow show, fully realised its equal application to the affairs of life. The Odes to Psyche and to Melancholy are metaphysically rather a relapse than an advance. The one is a very perfect example of imagery cultivated for its own sake, rather than as symbolic of any idea; the other expresses the deep sentimental melancholy which follows an extremity of instinctive joy, as night follows day, and satiety pursues excess.

> " Ay, in the very temple of delight
> Veil'd Melancholy keeps her sovran shrine,
> Though seen of none save him whose strenuous tongue
> Can burst Joy's grape against his palate fine."

Lamia, too, which he wrote next, is seriously compromised in its climax by the artificial conflict of philosophy and love—

> " Do not all charms fly
> At the mere touch of cold philosophy ? "

For, although we can accept the withering away of *Lamia,* representing sensuous love, beneath the potent truth of Apollonius' eye, the destruction of Lycius is an intolerable denial of reason. It is falsehood alone that truth kills, and Lycius should only have been the more vitally alive for being freed from the poison of his delusion. That he should die of such poison is intelligible, but not of its cure. There are passages in the poem too in Keats's worst manner—

> " He, sick to lose
> The amorous promise of her lone complain,
> Swoon'd murmuring of love, and pale with pain,"

and those other lines, perhaps the vulgarest, he ever wrote :

> " Let the mad poets say whate'er they please
> Of the sweets of Fairies, Peris, Goddesses,
> There is not such a treat among them all,
> Haunters of cavern, lake and waterfall,
> As a real woman, lineal indeed
> From Pyrrha's pebbles or old Adam's seed."

The advance here is not in taste or truth, but in power. Keats had shaken off the sweet lassitude of *The Eve of St. Agnes.* There was proof of new health in his very capacity to be energetically, assertively vulgar. He was preparing for active effort on a higher plane, and he trained his muscles on the lower. The construction of *Lamia* is his own; he may have trained his hands by a study of Milton and Dryden, but he is not here threading a texture on to a borrowed loom. The structure rises as he casts brick upon brick, and it is built with strength and determination. Alone of the narrative poems does it show a continuous and uncomplicated progress, an absence of stagnation. And this shows that Keats's mind had asserted itself, not as yet philosophically, for that entails depth as well as motion, but actively with the consequent control over the temptations to pleasurable indulgence by a consistent consciousness, which has an end in view. The surface of the sea is in motion, the deeps will inevitably follow, nay, they were already stirring; for he was even now at work upon the recast of *Hyperion*.

For one moment, as the autumn of this last year of unthreatened activity drew on, he turned once again to Nature, and gave himself wholly to her mood. The brightness which, we are told, graced the last days of that lingering summer, must have helped to soothe his spirit hovering distraught in the two worlds of life and art, between the turbulence of passion and the serenity of understanding. Much of its Sabbath calm, of its western sunlight, is pressed into the fragment, *The Eve of St. Mark*, but all the ripeness and resignation of the season, without a touch of langour or a tremor of excess, is embodied in the lines *To Autumn*. In Keats, too, the autumn of the body was surely come, not in any mere physical sense, although even there the winter of disease was close at hand, but in the implication that the monopoly of the body, so far as his poetry was concerned, was at an end. He had tasted the season's difference, and he knew that for one who pursued no other aim as a poet, only winter and death remained. He had wantoned with Spring and with Summer in all their moods, but the Autumn he wed in all faithfulness.

> "Where are the songs of Spring? Ay, where are they?
> Think not of them, thou hast they music too,
> While barrèd clouds bloom the soft-dying day,
> And touch the stubble-plains with rosy hue;
> Then in a wailful choir the small gnats mourn
> Among the river sallows, borne aloft
> Or sinking as the light wind lives or dies;
> And full-grown lambs loud bleat from hilly bourn;
> Hedge-crickets sing; and now with treble soft
> The red-breast whistles from a garden-croft;
> And gathering swallows twitter in the skies."

Nature has never spoken more truly in the human tongue. Personality, with its whims and prejudices, never encroaches for a moment; it selects the essential images, by the assured light of its absolute sympathy, melts them into one another by the warm tenderness of human emotion, and sustains them on an unbroken wave of music by the measuring faculty of the human mind.

This is the pure truth of naturalism; for where Wordsworth and Shelley imposed on nature their human precepts, Keats drew from her in grateful submission her own message and her own idea. Nature is neither moral nor philosophic. She merely exists from sensation to sensation. Keats captured her in a fair mood, for he preferred pleasure to pain; and so essentially did he render her in her dying beauty that the picture remains true and absolute so long as the "season of mists and mellow fruitfulness" returns.

Such an exercise of mind over matter, such discrimination, and such execution are only less than supreme as an imaginative triumph, because nature herself supplies a material already in its externality so significant of beauty to human sensibility, that the poet has merely to select and reject her images as he translates nature's poem into a new language. He doubtless translates with such perfection because his senses are in complete sympathy with her mood, of which inevitably her own images are the true expression. But this is a reflection of nature by man, as of a mother's beauty in the face of her son; it is not the direct utterance of his distinctive humanity. It is therefore only ideal because it is an absolute reading of a given moment in time, and seems to transcend material limits, and to figure to man the principles of eternity. But the imaginative effort required to record such a moment in a daylight world is less than that needed to clothe in adequate imagery the limitless aspirations and the searching vision of the human soul; it is less than that which can struggle with the agony of human life and defeat the darkness of death.

KEATS

The Romantic reaction against the mental conceit and the emotional poverty of the XVIII century lay in two directions.

It impelled men towards nature and towards humanity, and from the expression of the fact of both, to a pursuit of their truth.

The sequence was no doubt necessary, but it entailed considerable confusion as to what the aim of poetry was, and Wordsworth, while as yet unreproved by Coleridge, could suppose that a strict conformity with the speech and incidents of actual life constituted in itself poetic reality. To go back to life, to fling away the phrases and attitudes of a scholastic clique or a social class, was the first incident of a return to health; for true idealism can only grow out of the soil of impartial realism, but great poetry lies in the imaginative reading of the fact, not in the fact itself.

In Keats the two impulses are very clear, both in his attitude to nature and to man. We have marked his development from a luxurious surrender of his sensations to natural beauty, to a disciplined control, by which he rendered the loveliness of nature with that perfect economy of richness, that absolute harmony between the elements chosen, which reflects on a higher plane the self-destructive process of nature herself. He had attained therefore to nature's ideal, by following her methods. His attitude to man and even more to woman had been essentially similar. Towards mankind in general he had from the beginning shown a generous sympathy, but it was at bottom sentimental and vague, being inevitably unrelated to experience, and rather selfish in quality, since it caused him pleasure and gratification, by enlarging temporarily the radius of his own ego, without entailing any effort. His attitude to women was identical with his naturalism in its most indulgent form.* Their human personality does not exist for him, but he views them externally as graceful objects which excite desire. And this trivial instinct he had never up to this point either refined or deepened, as he had his other naturalistic impulses. We have already illustrated this in *Lamia*, and in the *Ode to Melancholy* we find him enjoying his mistress's pain or anger, with the spectatorial relish of one who views a passing rain-storm with its fine effect of trailing cloud. Doubtless woman, being a combined image of nature and humanity, a more natural and less intellectual creature than man, remained outside the refining process which is everywhere else visible in his naturalism. Her particular embodiment of nature would also hold his senses in far more narrow a captivity than even the physical world through which they found a comparative liberty.

Yet assuredly these stages of struggling self-

* Compare letter lxxxv.
' I never forget you, except after seeing now and then some beautiful woman—*but that is a fever.*'

realisation which we have traced are not to be deplored by any man, perfect as they are in the expression which Keats gave to them. Never did immaturity express itself more richly, or exploit its limitations to more purpose. The poetry of sense is a noble thing; it answers to our needs while we too are in the unpondered morning of our days; to our physical cravings, to our proud consciousness of sonship with earth, Keats gives ideal speech. In the very act, too, of cultivating his instinct, he was changing its office in the constiution of his powers; he was preparing it for the time when it would serve high intellectual purposes; in discovering the perfect form for embodying sensuous perception, he was evolving a technique which would answer later to the reality of a deeper experience, which would define that abstract idea of truth that hovered still hazy and nebulous in the subconscious depths of his mind.

In short, as he discriminated between instincts, his mental powers grew in strength. While the senses are all-powerful, the mind either slumbers, or it exercises itself on the surface of reality, in fancy, and in technical cunning.

> " Ever let the Fancy roam,
> Pleasure never is at home :
> At a touch sweet pleasure melteth,
> Like to bubbles when rain pelteth ;
> Then let winged Fancy wander
> Though the thought still spread beyond her,"

and

" Oh, sweet Fancy! let her loose;
Everything is spoilt by use:
Where's the cheek that doth not fade,
Too much gaz'd at? Where's the maid
Whose lip mature is ever new?
Where's the eye, however blue,
Doth not weary? Where's the face
One would meet in every place?
Where's the voice, however soft,
One would hear so very oft? "

It is no more than pretty triviality. But as the mind learns to rule the senses at its discretion, it turns to the facts of life, seeking to discriminate there also the false, or trivial, from the true, or essential. It seeks knowledge, and its first discovery is that in humanity lies a world interpenetrated by, but distinct from nature. A poet approaches humanity with the same sympathy which drew him to nature, but with more mind, because man is an abstraction which does not immediately excite bodily pleasure, but rather philosophic curiosity, and philanthropic desire.* Keats had sought and found pleasure through desire; he now turned and pursued truth through love. Nature is become the hand-maiden, not his

---

* Compare letter lv.
The familiar passage concerning the 'Thoughtless Chamber' and the Chamber of ' Maiden Thought,' leading up to—
' However among the effects this breathing is father of is that tremendous one of sharpening one's vision into the heart and nature of Man—of convincing one's nerves that the world is full of Misery, Heart-break, Pain, Sickness, and oppression. Whereby this Chamber of Maiden Thought becomes gradually darkened, and at the same time, on all sides of it, many doors are set open— but all dark—all leading to dark passages. . . . . . Now if we live, and go on thinking, we too shall explore them.'

mistress—mind his sovereign, not his plaything; fancy is changing into imagination, and an imagination so evolved will assuredly not want for a physical vocabulary.

xi

Keats was at work on *Hyperion* and *The Eve of St. Agnes* at the same time. In the one he was reducing his sensations to a perfect form of art, in the other he was trying to embody the conception that for the world at large a dispensation of art must replace a dispensation of nature. It has been said that the imaginative idea in the first version of *Hyperion,* is tenuous, and that Keats abandoned it for that reason. With this we cannot agree: the idea is powerful and original, and he abandoned the poem chiefly because he had adopted a form for expressing it which tempted him into imagery for imagery's sake, and which he rightly believed to be endangering the direct appeal and expression of the idea. That a poem which preached the evolution of nature into art, rather than the denial of nature by art, should in its form offer anywhere an example of " art for art's sake," was a contradiction which he was too genuine to tolerate.

Hyperion in its first version embodies the conception that " Beauty is Truth," in its second, that " Truth is Beauty "—a conviction which Keats only arrived at after he had drawn from nature all the pure beauty which she has in her to offer, and had

93

turned from her to knowledge and to man in search
of a higher truth and a purer idea.

Yet the first version is extremely significant, because Keats, in the act of creating it, forced into
the full daylight of his mind the principle upon
which he was acting when he wrote *The Eve of St.
Agnes* or the *Ode to Autumn*, namely, the submission
of the sensations received from nature to the dict-
tatorship of selective reason. And he learnt from it
therefore that the natural world offers but a limited
and humble province for the vast forces of human
reason to work upon, and that

> " to bear all naked truths,
> And to envisage circumstance, all calm,
> That is the top of sovereignty."

It is notable also that each of the forms of life
typified in *Endymion* as the natural beauty of Earth,
the fire of the regions under the Earth, the forces of
death under the Sea, the spiritual life of the Air, re-
appear in *Hyperion* under different symbols and in
a new relationship.

But we need not here enter in detail into the
mythology, or into the incidents of the poem; wishing only to relate them to the development of Keats's
own imagination. For *Hyperion* is primarily an
expression of its author's feelings and of the poetical
dilemma with which he was faced. It was indeed
only abandoned because the cumbersome machinery
was getting out of hand and going its own involved

mythological way, to the confusion and entangle-
ment of Keats's own desire for self-expression. At
the same time his continual emphasis of his own
immediate personal philosophy on the lips of his
characters was destroying any of the balancing contrast between the old and new dispensations, which
the incidents were supposed to figure.

Hyperion and Apollo are not, as they should be, re-
spectively sons of darkness and of light : they are
twin brothers, because they represent two succeeding
moments in Keats's mind. Yet in the fallen Titans
Keats meant to embody the forces of nature, Saturn
being the first born of parental darkness, out of which
came Earth or Thea, and Hyperion the Light or essential fire, germinated from matter as the spark from the
friction of flint and stone. And from the merging of
fire and matter came life, and of life came man.
Oceanus is the symbol of material senseless death,
and Apollo of human activity and human intelligence, and the metaphysical argument of the poem
is briefly that the Kingdom of Earth and of natural
law must pass, to be replaced by that of Spirit and
of the ideal reason which is Love. Saturn is the
power which penetrates the whole atomic universe.
He is not mind set above matter, but the inexhaust-
ible force of creative and destructive energy. He is
the elemental universe in the equilibrium of its
perpetual motion. Reduced to earth, he is function-
less. He is like a great organ compressed, if such
were possible, into one of its own pipes. His only

creative conception is endlessly to destroy and out of
the ruins to shape again, following the law of nature,
not of intelligence.

> " But cannot I create ?
> Cannot I form ?   Cannot I fashion forth
> Another world, another universe,
> To overbear and crumble this to nought ?
> Where is another chaos ?   Where ? "

He cannot form, save out of dissolution.

On earth, too, which is understood to be the earth
of men, Fate had poured on him a " mortal oil, a
disannointing poison," which exposes him to all the
fraility of human weaknesses, grief, fears, passions,
hopes and despairs, without the safeguard of a human
intelligence.   He is conscious of the evils of sensation, without having the power to set them right.

He contrasts his material stature with the puny
build of mortals, and cannot comprehend why

> " The firstborn of all shaped and palpable gods
> Should cower beneath what in comparison
> Is untremendous might . . "

Saturn's dilemma is that of the sensationalist in a
world of imperfectly realised intellectual values, of
the body in the audit chamber of the mind : he
approaches a reflection of Keats himself when on the
full stream of his instinct he floated through *Endymion*.   *Hyperion*, however, is an even exacter repre-
sentation. He alone of the old natural dynasty retains

his sovereignty, but in dismay and distraction, because " omens dread fright and perplex him," and instead of sweet incense rising from the earth, a " savour of poisonous brass and metal sick " and the sound of " neighing steeds " creeps in to his bright palace to visit him with a sense of horror. These symbolise the agonies and strifes of the human world.

> " O dreams of day and night !
> O monstrous forms ! O effigies of pain !
> O spectres busy in a cold, cold gloom !
> O lank-eared Phantoms of black-weeded pools !
> Why do I know ye ? Why have I seen ye ? Why
> Is my eternal essence thus distraught
> To see and to behold these horrors new ?
> Saturn is fallen, am I too to fall ?
> Am I to leave this haven of my rest,
> This cradle of my glory, this soft clime,
> This calm luxuriance of blissful light,
> These crystalline pavilions and pure fanes
> Of all my lucent empire ? It is left
> Deserted, void, nor any haunt of mine.
> The blaze, the splendour and the symmetry,
> I cannot see—but darkness, death and darkness,
> Even here, into my centre of repose,
> The shady visions come to domineer,
> Insult and blind, and stifle up my pomp."

Hyperion is the fiery essence, as distinct from the matter of nature : his has been a luxurious life in the circulating sap and the tingling sunlight of earth. He is the male element in creation, the natural idea : Thea is the female, the natural matter.

But the poem stages the moment when man's formative capacity challenges nature's; man both possesses a fire of his own, and can control the fire of nature. It is indeed the smoke of his fires, of his wars and agonies floating in the void, that Hyperion saw.

> " A mist arose, as from a scummy marsh.
> At this, through all his bulk an agony
> Crept gradual."

In *Hyperion* Keats envisages very accurately himself, and in allowing Hyperion almost human attributes, he seriously impairs his significance as a merely natural force. For Keats, too, had wed the earth, as Hyperion wed Thea. He, too, had lived in all "the blaze, the splendour, and the symmetry" of that unviolated palace of the natural world, and upon him the darkness of the knowledge of pain was falling, to discredit his natural impulses, and compel a new endeavour. He, like

> " the bright Titan, phrenzied with new woes,
> Unus'd to bend, by hard compulsion bent
> His spirit to the sorrow of the time."

The advice which Coelus offers to Hyperion at the end of the first book might well represent the philosophic part of Keats addressing the sensuous. For Hyperion, despite his doomed incapacity to escape his natural limitations, is not only the fiery essence of life in fact, but has also an ideal significance. He is one of those

KEATS

"symbols divine,
Manifestations of that beauteous life
Diffus'd unseen throughout eternal space."

He is the truth which Keats had sensed in nature
and eternalised in art; he is the creative principle of
life. But Keats, in his desire to express himself,
attaches to Hyperion also other qualities which cannot in reason belong to a natural force, and gravely
complicate the argument of the poem. Matter acts
upon matter, but it is incapable of knowing matter,
still less the things of the mind and the spirit. Yet
unlike Coelus, who is but a voice, whose life is

"but the life of winds and tides,
No more than winds and tides can I avail."

Hyperion is figured like Saturn as conscious of the
passions of men. He does not merely exist in pure
unconscious self-absorption; rather he is urged to
make use of his elemental power and his consciousness of the new activities of life to "be in the van of
circumstance." This corresponds to the duty which
Keats imposed on himself when he wrote "that he
must get knowledge and understanding." Hyperion
cannot succeed as Keats can in his creative struggle,
because, though conscious of the new forces gathered
against him, he has not the mind by which alone he
could defeat mind.

Oceanus, versed in the secrets of death, pronounces
the cause of the assured doom of the Titans with a

noble stoicism, and a fine appreciation of evolution-
ary necessity. He has wandered through the avenue
of death to eternal truth, and

> " Now comes the pain of death, to whom 'tis pain;
> We fall by course of nature's law, not force
> Of thunder or of Jove."

As parental Darkness sprang out of Chaos, and as
Light gave life to the Heaven and the Earth, and
the Titans themselves were evolved, and

> " As Heaven and Earth are fairer, fairer far
> Than Chaos and blank Darkness, though once chiefs;
> And as we show beyond that Heaven and Earth
> In form and shape compact and beautiful,
> In will, in action free, companionship,
> And thousand other signs of purer life;
> So on our heels a fresh perfection treads,
> A power more strong in beauty, born of us,
> And fated to excel us as we pass
> In glory, that old Darkness: nor are we
> Thereby more conquer'd, than by us the rule
> Of shapeless Chaos."

The process of nature is continual creation, in which
the physically strong survives, if only for its season.
In her mind is latent, as the economy of her forces.
But out of the strong is come forth sweetness, out of
the body is come the conscious mind, examining the
selfish instincts and imposing a new law and a new
valuation. Those who supersede the Titans, as
Oceanus says, do it in right of their beauty, which is
strength governed by reason,

" for 'tis the eternal law
That first in beauty should be first in might.
Yea, by that law, another race may drive
Our conquerors to mourn as we do now.
Have ye beheld the young God of the Seas,
My dispossessor? Have ye seen his face?
. . I saw him on the calméd waters scud,
With such a glow of beauty in his eyes,
That it enforc'd me to bid sad farewell
To all my empire."

The argument is clear enough. The first manifestation of spiritual beauty is doubtless imperfect: yet it dispossesses the rule of natural forces, because, however uncertainly, reason has begun to control instinct, and creation is no longer a blind process: the human soul exists, an eternal law has displaced a natural, and what development there is will represent only an enlargement of the powers of reason, until the ugly offspring of instinct with their destructive lusts cease to exist, in a world created and governed by pure love.

Oceanus' daughter Clymene states the case even more explicitly. For her too the old natural joy is lost in the knowledge of woe. And to ease her heart she takes a shell from the seashore, and murmurs into it and makes melody, when suddenly

" There came enchantment with the shifting wind,
That did both drown and keep alive my ears.
I threw my shell away upon the sand,
And a wave fill'd it, as my sense was fill'd
With that new blissful golden melody."

It was the music of Apollo. And here Keats has brought into direct antagonism the beauty of art and of nature. Apollo's is the music of the human soul, as distinct from the lyrical note of the sea or the waterfall, and it conquers because it is not an accident of natural forces, unaware of their own momentary harmony. Yet it is possible that this art of Apollo, as Keats first conceived it, was indeed an "art for art's sake." We have said that Keats in his first version had attained to the conception that "Beauty is truth," rather than to its converse. And the music of Apollo, in which "a living death was in each gust of sounds," was of that luxurious tone which Keats produced in his own *Ode to a Nightingale*. It was sensuousness made conscious and perfect; it lacked the passion of truth finding a beauteous form for itself. This supposition is confirmed by the fragment of the last book.

Here we are shown the meeting of Apollo and the Titaness Mnemosyne. Critics have often taken it for a weakness and confusion in Keats's mind that he introduces these two weeping and raving, supposing that Apollo should be confident and radiant in the strength of his new power and purpose. This arises, we think, from a mistaken view of Apollo's significance. Once again it is the Keats of the moment who is personified in Apollo, and Mnemosyne, although she has forsaken the Titans to instruct him, is still a Titaness, and her memory relates only to the aeons of the natural world; she is not of the new dispensation. She can give him knowledge, and madden him with the passion of it; she cannot teach him how to use it. She can only fill his young mind, straining at particles of light, with the facts and the experiences of the old dispensation. Hers is the lore of that nature to which Keats had surrendered his instinct. He can deliver himself up to her and taste a momentary material ecstasy, as he has done so constantly,

> " Knowledge enormous makes a god of me.
> Names, deeds, grey legends, dire events rebellious,
> Majesties, sovran voices, agonies,
> Creations and destroyings, all at once
> Pour into the wide hollows of my brain,
> And deify me, as if some blithe wine
> Or bright elixir peerless I had drunk,
> And so become immortal."

It is as if here all his moments of spontaneous abandonment to life and its convulsive mystery broke upon his mind simultaneously, like a great flood of many waves, and overwhelmed his consciousness. Mnemosyne is the Memory of all his instinctive ecstasy in nature, as he had realised it from his earliest efforts in poetry up to this moment. She is the mother of his young and ardent muse; she nursed his boyhood, but she cannot assist or prevent the manhood on the threshold of which he now stands.

> " For me, dark, dark,
> And painful vile oblivion seals my eyes:
> I strive to search wherefore I am so sad,
> Until a melancholy numbs my limbs;
> And then upon the grass I sit, and mourn
> Like one who once had wings . .
> Are there not other regions than this isle?
> What are the stars? "

Mnemosyne could never have enlightened him. It was not within the scope of her experience. She belonged to the kingdom of physical force and physical pleasure, which was passing away. She is the servant of necessity.

But in Apollo Keats stands plain to see, with his young reason straining out into the darkness of life, which he has not yet the power to illuminate, with his senses tasting their first disillusionment, and their first profound apathy, as he realises that the isle on which he has pastured for so long is but a narrow strip of land, where Calibans and Circes lurk amid the flowers, and that there is a wider province to be attained only by the soaring soul, by impassioned imagination seeking acquaintance with the stars themselves, in its quest for the last liberty of absolute enlightenment.

xii

Hyperion was abandoned as much because the manner and the mythology were strangling the idea, as because the idea was confusing and rendering inconsequent the mythology. Perhaps an even deeper reason however was that Keats himself shared the darkness of Apollo, and discovered that Mnemosyne could not enlighten him. He had exaggerated the virtue and capacity of " the old dispensation," and he could not yet vision clearly the new. The two had mingled confusedly in his mind, the appeal of nature to his senses and the appeal of truth to his reason, and only after writing *Hyperion* did he discover their absolute distinction in kind.

In his ambiguity he had made the Titans too benign, and Apollo too much a reflection of himself when he was cultivating art and nature for their own sake. The destructive fact of nature, her dull brutality, is as little typified in Saturn, as the constructive idea is to be found in Apollo. Natural life in the persons of the Titans is sentimentalised, and the function of art is restricted to extricating the intensest sweets from nature, and to the making of her spontaneous music into a " golden melody."

This was the point which Keats had reached when he wrote *The Eve of St. Agnes*. It was on the passive memory of Mnemosyne that he drew for all the images amid which he luxuriated there. But the new dispensation, if it was to offer any contrast to the old, would have to reveal a power of mind " envisaging circumstance," apprehending truth beyond the range of the senses, and satisfying the needs and the mute questions of humanity. For this Keats realised he was still incompetent. He could draw on the memory of his senses, he could recall past experience and beautify it, he could not reason out the present, nor peer through the cloud portals of the future. His reason was still unequal to the task; active imagination was still withheld. He could not, in short, employ the riches, which he had won from nature, to image a coherent human idea.

Yet in *Hyperion* Keats had discovered and imperfectly voiced one profound truth. He had realised that nature offers a varied spectacle of forces, not merely to be enjoyed or passively reflected by a poet, but to be used by an inspired intelligence for the creation of unadulterated beauty, in perpetual harmony with the soul of man, because it satisfies his rational as well as his sensuous perception. Nature he had discovered to be as disinterestedly destructive as creative. He had foreseen the Darwinian hypothesis. But he had denied its application to men. It was for them, and for the poet, as their ideal voice, to replace the disinterestedness of natural law by that of love,* by an understanding which, seeing into the truth of things, realised the causes of error and wrong as clearly as those of wisdom and virtue, and wished therefore not to destroy anything, but rather to demonstrate to Ugliness the path by which

---

* Compare letter cvi. Passage beginning
‘ Very few men have even arrived at a complete disinterestedness of Mind . . . . . .

. . . . . . Do you not think I strive to know myself? ’ This passage is of high significance. In it Keats contrasts a natural with a Human morality.

it might attain to Beauty. It was a conviction of this as the true duty of the poet, to be a sage physician of human ill, that Keats expresses in the revised induction, and which leads him to his culminating apprehension of reality in Moneta.

From nature herself he had learned the inestimable lesson that creation, which is all life truly lived, implies positive action, a constant resolving of discord into harmony, and that the poet's function was to emulate her process on a higher plane, to substitute a world of pure intelligence for one of pure force. The effort required to mount from the dreamer to the seer was severe, but he made it, and he succeeded.

xiii

In the few months which intervened before he was definitely at work on the revision, he had been writing the Odes and *Lamia,* and his mind had developed a consciousness of its own powers, while in the *Ode to Autumn* we may well believe that he had touched the absolute truth of nature, and realised that there was no further advance possible along that path. When therefore in the September of that same year he turned to write the *Fall of Hyperion,* he had for the first time made the idea which had so long vaguely eluded him sufficiently his own to demand a directer expression.

The problem before him was to discover a structure which would most nearly express the urgent conviction possessing his mind, without interposing any material, however beautiful in itself, between the idea and its inevitable form. The ponderous objectivity of the first version, like the involved allegory of *Endymion*, was due to a lack of definition in the idea. In the revision Keats himself speaks, he commands the argument and the scene. He is no longer swept away on the current of an invading life,

> ' Since every man whose soul is not a clod
> Hath visions and would speak, if he had lov'd,
> And been well nurtur'd in his mother tongue."

The poem represents very accurately the philosophical conviction which Keats now possessed. He understood finally what the highest aim of poetry entailed. Momentary aspiration mounting on the wings of emotion, as it did in the Odes, was not enough. The savage guessing at heaven, the fanatic weaving his paradisal dream, do but trace the shadows of truth which must either surrender to the darkness or yield to the full sunlight.

He describes his own early intercourse with the beauties of nature, in a fair garden where a feast of summer fruits was spread, and how he ate deliciously " and, after not long, thirsted." He drank from " a cool vessel of transparent juice," which signifies poetry, as he for so long conceived it, and in vain struggling against the domineering potion " the cloudy swoon came on, and down I sank." This of course signifies all the intoxication of his young

naturalism. But such intoxication he understands
to be only the first manifestation of poetic sensibility.
For

"That full draught is parent of my theme."

He wakes in a sanctuary, a place of ruin and grey
antiquity, symbolising the pain of all the ages with
which he sympathises, and its secrets are those of
all knowledge, of all the facts of life through which
the mind of man attains to truth. The columns north
and south end in mist of nothing, that is in the
innumerable facts of the past which the mind of man
can never learn; in the east, the lost Paradise of
man's natural state, "black gates were shut against
the sunrise evermore." But in the west, the future
towards which he and man must move, he sees far
off an altar beneath "An image huge of feature as a
cloud." This altar represents Truth, the leaves burning upon it the years of human life, and the steps
leading up to it, which he climbs with infinite
difficulty, are the processes of thought by which a
man must struggle from the apprehension of fact to
that of Truth.

"If thou canst not ascend
These steps, die on that marble where thou art.
Thy flesh, near cousin to the common dust,
Will parch for lack of nutriment."

They who perceive only the facts of life, whether by
their senses or their mind, are subject to the natural

law of fact, which is death. We might even suppose that Keats foresaw his own early death, when he says :

"The sands of thy short life are spent this hour,"

and felt the burning need of climbing in time beyond the material world into the ideal. He strives desperately against the increasing numbness and suffocation, and

"One minute before death, my ic'd foot touch'd
The lowest stair ; and as it touch'd, life seem'd
To pour in at the toes."

Moneta, the veiled shadow, distinct from Mnemosyne of the previous version, is a symbol not of passive Memory, but of active Experience. She is the priestess of all knowledge and absolute reality, not the repository of past sensations. She can inform a poet both of the facts and the truth of human life, not merely of nature's " creations and destroyings."

"None can usurp this height," returned that shade,
" But those to whom the miseries of the world
Are misery, and will not let them rest.
All else who find a haven in the world,
Where they may thoughtless sleep away their days,
If by a chance into this fane they come,
Rot on the pavement where thou rottedst half."
" Are there not thousands in the world," said I,
Encourag'd by the sooth voice of the shade,
" Who love their fellows even to the death,
Who feel the giant agony of the world,
And more, like slaves to poor humanity,

Labour for mortal good? I sure should see
Other men here, but I am here alone."
" Those whom thou spak'st of are no visionaries,"
Rejoin'd that voice—" they are no dreamers weak;
They seek no wonder but the human face,
No music but a happy-noted voice—
They come not here, they have no thought to come—
And thou art here, for thou are less than they."

It has been inferred from this passage that Keats
values above the poet not only the lovers of humanity, but the purely animal and unthinking man,
because he shares in the actions of life and accepts
its joy or pain. This is only true if we define what
Keats meant by " poet " at this point. He is a
dreaming thing, a fever of himself, who " venoms all
his days." Moneta is addressing a poet who has but
now escaped from sensual death, who stands on the
lowest of those steps which lead to truth, who in the
loss of his instinctive power and the immaturity of
his rational, may well be distraught with dreams and
exhausted with fever. But he is only less than those
who accept the world at its face value and are therefore to that extent true to life, because having rejected
a physical world he is as yet too weak to relate himself to a spiritual. Before him, however, lies an
infinite province, a boundless liberty, if he have the
courage to go forward.

Keats then uses the word visionary here as synony-
mous with dreamer, and he implies by it one who has
realised the insufficiency of sense, but has not yet

developed a power of reason capable of envisaging the world of nature and of man and drawing from it its truth; and who therefore employs his mind in the creation of weak fantasies, bearing no relation to reality. This is the poet of selfish dilettantism, of " art for art's sake " whom Keats knew himself to have been at times. But he continues:

> " If it please,
> Majestic shadow, tell me : sure not all
> Those melodies sung into the world's ear
> Are useless ; sure a poet is a sage ;
> A humanist, physician to all men.
> That I am none I feel, as vultures feel
> They are no birds when eagles are abroad.
> What am I then ? "

Keats understands now the scope of the true poet, and he admits his own present inability to pretend to it. For Moneta answers:

> " Art thou not of the dreamer tribe ?
> The poet and the dreamer are distinct,
> Diverse, sheer opposite, antipodes.
> The one pours out a balm upon the world,
> The other vexes it."

The dreamer merely soothes the pain of the world with the poetry of exquisite pleasure, the poet vexes it, because by revealing the truth, he excites men to discard all that is false in their actions, or at least to regard a misguided and material life with disgust and anger. Keats at these words invokes Apollo to destroy

" all mock lyrists, large self-worshippers,
And careless Hectorers in proud bad verse,
Though I breathe death with them, it will be life
To see them sprawl before me into graves."

And in thus discarding all that is false or self-absorbed or trivial, he enters upon the vision of reality which is the end of all his striving. Moneta unveils herself and tells him that

" the scenes
Still swooning vivid through my globed brain
With an electral changing misery,
Thou shalt with these dull mortal eyes behold
Free from all pain, if wonder pain thee not."

And thus he sees her

" Then saw I a wan face,
Not pin'd by human sorrows, but bright-blanch'd
By an immortal sickness which kills not;
It works a constant change, which happy death
Can put no end to; deathwards progressing
To no death was that visage; it had passed
The lily and the snow; and beyond these
I must not think now, though I saw that face.
But for her eyes I should have fled away.
They held me back with a benignant light,
Soft mitigated by divinest lids
Half-clos'd, and visionless entire they seem'd
Of all external things—they saw me not,
But, in blank splendour, beam'd like the mild moon,
Who comforts those she sees not, who knows not
What eyes are upward cast."

Keats has attained at last to the idea, the central reality, into which all the sensations of life are gathered, in which gladness and sorrow, life and death, lose those attributes of contrast conditioned by earth, in which the passion, whether of hatred or of love is soothed and mitigated into a union of benignant light. Good and evil are become one, not in a realistic surrender of distinction, but in ideal reconcilement, in the liberty of Love.*

Moneta's eyes that held him, beaming "like the mild moon," were the same which he sought but never found in the luxuriant world of *Endymion*, bathed in misty moonlight. He has seen them and imaged them now, and we can be certain that he could never again have looked on the world with the eyes of a material lover.

One who had pierced through all circumstance to that first principle of being, that synthesis of opposites, and expressed it not as an abstraction, but as a concrete figure appreciable to the senses, could never take delight again in the mere externals of life. For in the assurance of that revelation

> " there grew
> A power within me of enormous ken.
> To see as a God sees, and take the depth
> Of things as nimbly as the outward eye
> Can size and shape pervade."

*Compare letter xxvi.
' The excellence of every art is its intensity, capable of making all disagreeables evaporate from their being in close relationship with Beauty and Truth.'

How he would have expressed that reality we cannot say. But with the whole world of men through all the ages lying ready to his hand, and with his own unrivalled mastery of language and imagery, learnt in the school of nature, he could not have failed to embody adequately, whether in the drama as he hoped, or in epic or narrative verse, the truth which his proud imagination guaranteed to him. That he could have succeeded fully in the *Fall of Hyperion* is doubtful; for he was trying to graft on to his new vision of reality a structure which he had created before he was fully aware of the power and the responsibility of his imagination. And what he still lacked was a knowledge of worldly fact for his now sincere imagination to work upon. He had reached the truth by passionate intuition, he needed now to return in the assurance of his vision to the world in which previously he had too blindly luxuriated, and from which he had fled in the troubled discontent of awakening reason.

Nature, he had perceived, has constantly betrayed the heart that loved her without discrimination, and in his last days he knew it to be the poet's highest duty to enter by a sympathetic understanding into the life not only of nature but of man, and by that complete identification with the universe, that " fellowship with essence," win the power to vision for man a world of higher harmonies. To the intuition of reality he had won, he had completed his identity with truth. He needed only experience and knowledge, human and intellectual, of men and affairs, on which to exercise the passionate psychology which imaginative understanding represents. His intuition would then have not only pierced through at the central point of life to the reality beyond, but would have perforated, if we may use the expression, the whole shell of existence which lay before him to observe. We can imagine to what noble uses an intuition, which had already discriminated so finely between the complicated impressions of sense, would have turned such necessary experiences.

He would surely then have stood with Shakespeare, in right of more than universal accomplishment foreshadowed. And as we view with sadness the too brief morning of the XIX century, which was to be followed by so long and indolent a noontide, and an evening unreal with the suffocation and lassitude of thunder, here and there with stray flashes of protesting lightning, we cannot but lament Keats's death with a poignancy that even the author of *Adonais* could not realise.

For the idealism of the Romantic movement failed so speedily because it was not sufficiently rooted in the earth. It outgrew its strength, and stretching upward to the remote heavens, it withered at its base. The idealism which is going to persist and to influence poetry so profoundly that it can with difficulty accept again a material or a superficial view of life, must itself grow out of life, and raise life up to its own conception of truth, freeing it of all baser substance.

It is this process which we have traced in Keats himself, a gradual enlightenment of the spirit from within, a measured advance in which there are no sudden leaps and bounds, and no traversing of easy roads or impatient overstepping of morasses to a difficult goal. His sensuousness is not to be regretted or condoned; it is to be accepted as a fact inevitable to the full maturing of a noble genius. Without an experience of fact and a fine animal faculty, the truth to which we attain is necessarily an abstraction, nebulous in itself, or applied mistakenly from outside to circumstances to which it does not rightly belong. The truth and the fact, the ideal and the real must coincide, and the only certain way of making them coincide is to evolve the one out of the other. This both Shelley and Wordsworth, both Coleridge and Byron, rarely accomplished. Shelley's ideas were absolute enough, but they were born of philosophic speculation, and in the rare instances when he applied them to a material life of which he was divinely ignorant, the union was strained and sometimes incongruous. Wordsworth had originally the animal sympathy, sometimes conducive to an intimacy with fact, but circumstances hindered its natural development, and his mental powers being in themselves limited, his philosophy soon hardened into dogma, and his idealism into moralising. Coleridge was ever too transcendental, and he lacked the will for persistent effort. Byron possessed the energy and the imagination, but he was born into an artificial life and wasted his powers on exposing the hypocrisies of a class, and relieving his own spleen at its expense.

In Keats alone do we find all the qualities necessary to comprehensive genius, the passion, the mind and the will, unspoiled by class prejudice or the pedantries of academic learning.

The result of education on an intellectual youth is too often to prevent him reaping the natural harvest of life by feeding him on the forced fruits of learning. Even this Keats had avoided. He went to school to life; he learnt by disillusionment and self-recrimination, by being guilty of vulgarities and regretting them, by tasting pleasure and satiety. The idealism which he would have embodied had he lived would not have died for want of sustenance, or gone up in smoke. It would have been built out of the granite of earth herself, and watered with the dew of heaven. Dying as he did, on the very threshold of absolute truth, it was inevitable that the work, perfect in its kind, in which he idealised or even sentimentalised nature, should have unhealthily fascinated a generation which, caring more for Beauty than for Truth, allowed finally the element of falsehood, of selfishness in their conception to poison the very beauty which they loved.

Keats himself, as we have seen, was too searchingly honest to mistake the grace of sentiment for anything but a limited and selfish attainment, to be discarded as insufficient by all who sought to realise true manhood and absolute reality, or loved their fellows as they ought.

And there can be no question that the revised induction to *Hyperion* is the most profoundly beautiful and permanent of all his works, just because, in virtue of its absolute truth, it is removed out of the condition of time and set above the accident of circumstance. We cannot help conjecturing that the whole quality of Victorian poetry might have been different, had this magnificent fragment survived as the first example of his maturer powers, and had his earlier poems, like *Venus and Adonis* in the creative history of Shakespeare, fallen into their natural place, as the rich outpourings of a young and ardent sensibility, displaced, but not discredited, by something greater.

He who was caught into the tide of a generation reacting with extravagant justice against the complacence of a self-sufficient mentality, would surely, had he lived, have added to the rich liberation of sense which Romanticism claimed, the astringency of a Classic conscience.

xiv

We have confined ourselves in this brief study to tracing the stages by which Keats approached an absolute comprehension of truth, and of the poet's responsibility as typifying the truth. It is in the light of this ultimate idea, the culminating triumph of the human reason, that we have considered all his poetry and assessed its merits.

Yet no appreciation of Keats can be complete which fails to pay a tribute to his art as art. We have watched the growth of his mind, and we know that in splendid maturity it must have created for itself a body purer in its reflection of reality than that which his instinct conceived. Yet nature never begot more perfect children than he did poems in the many inspired moments of his buoyant youth. His human instinct was then in exact sympathy with the creative mind wedding the earth in spring, and although these Saturnian nuptials, this instinctive union with nature, are subject to the doom of death, while the Promethean lover weds the immortal soul of things that can never fade away, yet in the pure art which makes order out of confusion and regulates the self-destroying elements of a sensual chaos, there is apparent an exercise of mind over matter, however unconscious. Ideal realism is only one degree less absolute than creative idealism itself. For it repeats the creative triumph of nature in the ideal medium of language, where no destructive law brings night upon the day, nor dissolution to forms of beauty. Thus the butterfly which Keats saw fluttering in the ecstasy of its one brief day of sunlight lives surely as long as Englishmen and the tongue they speak survive.

" Lightly this little herald flew aloft,
Follow'd by glad Endymion's clasped hands :
Onward it flies. From languor's sullen bands
His limbs are loosed, and eager, on he hies
Dazzled to trace it in the sunny skies.
It seem'd he flew, the way so easy was ;
And like a new-born spirit did he pass
Through the green evening quiet in the sun,
O'er many a heath, through many a woodland dun,
Through buried paths, where sleepy twilight dreams
The summer time away. One track unseams
A wooded cleft, and, far away, the blue
Of ocean fades upon him ; then, anew,
He sinks adown a solitary glen,
Where there was never sound of mortal men,
Saving, perhaps, some snow-light cadences
Melting to silence, when upon the breeze
Some holy bark let forth an anthem sweet,
To cheer itself to Delphi."

That is the absolute truth of nature. Keats took
wing with the butterfly, saw the earth pass beneath
his feet, and made the unconscious momentary
journey into a thing of eternal experience. And in
those other imperfect moods in which he remains too
conscious of his own identity to lose himself wholly
in nature, or, lacking the power to relate himself
truly to her, returns from her to life with petulant
dissatisfaction, the felicity of his utterance rarely
fails ; his art as art is always perfect so long as he
feels passionately, however misdirected the feeling
may have been. Such art it is superfluous to praise,
and we honour Keats as he would have wished, by

accepting them as perfect in their divine limitations, and passing on, as he did himself, from the pleasure of the senses to the ecstasy of truth, from a material life, intense but fleeting, to a reality in the light of which the mutabilities of life cease to tantalise, because they are proved variations on a constant theme.

BIBLIOGRAPHY

THE COMPLETE WORKS OF JOHN KEATS, edited by H. Buxton Forman.

POEMS OF KEATS, edited with an introduction by Ernest de Sélincourt.

LIFE OF JOHN KEATS, by Sidney Colvin.

JOHN KEATS : A Critical Essay, by Robert Bridges.

JOHN KEATS : A Study, by F. M. Owen.

COLERIDGE : Biographia Literaria, Chapter xiii. ' On the Imagination.'

SCHILLER : Essays Aesthetical and Philosophical.

THE ROMANTIC MOVEMENT IN ENGLISH LITERATURE, by Arthur Symons.

Articles contained in the following :—

> ESSAYS IN CRITICISM, second series, by Matthew Arnold.
> THE ENGLISH POETS, by James Russell Lowell.
> OXFORD LECTURES ON POETRY, by A. C. Bradley.
> STUDIES AND ESSAYS, by Mary Suddard.
> WORDSWORTH, SHELLEY, KEATS, and other ESSAYS, by David Masson.

THE JOHN KEATS MEMORIAL VOLUME :

> Articles by Miss Amy Lowell, Mr. John Bailey, Professor Mackail, Dr. Herford, and particularly by Mr. Lascelles Abercrombie, Professor Ker, Dr. Andrew Bradley, Col. Arthur Lynch.

ARTICLES by Mr. John Middleton Murry, in *The Athenæum*, July, 25th, 1919; *The Nation and The Athenæum*, Feb. 26th, 1921.